Start With Radical Love

For my children: Zena, Kenzo, and Zora.
May you forever know me more through
the words on these pages.

Start With Radical Love

Antiracist Pedagogy for Social Justice Educators

Crystal Belle

For information:

Corwin
A SAGE Company
2455 Teller Road
Thousand Oaks, California 91320
(800) 233-9936
www.corwin.com

SAGE Publications Ltd.
1 Oliver's Yard
55 City Road
London EC1Y 1SP
United Kingdom

SAGE Publications India Pvt. Ltd.
Unit No 323-333, Third Floor, F-Block
International Trade Tower Nehru Place
New Delhi 110 019
India

SAGE Publications Asia-Pacific Pte. Ltd.
18 Cross Street #10-10/11/12
China Square Central
Singapore 048423

Vice President and Editorial Director:
Monica Eckman
Program Director and Publisher:
Dan Alpert
Acquisitions Editor: Megan Bedell
Content Development Editor: Mia
Rodriguez
Content Development Manager:
Lucas Schleicher
Senior Editorial Assistant:
Natalie Delpino
Production Editor: Vijayakumar
Copy Editor: Ritika Sharma
Typesetter: TNQ Technologies Pvt. Ltd.
Proofreader: Girish Kumar Sharma
Indexer: TNQ Technologies Pvt. Ltd.
Cover Designer: Scott Van Atta
Marketing Manager: Stephanie Trkay

Printed in the United States of America

Library of Congress Cataloging-in-Publication Data

Names: Belle, Crystal.

Title: Start with radical love : antiracist pedagogy for social justice educators / Crystal Belle.

Description: First edition. | Thousand Oaks, California : Corwin Press, [2024] | Includes bibliographical references and index.

Identifiers: LCCN 2023049312 | ISBN 9781071827710 (paperback : acid-free paper) | ISBN 9781071827680 (adobe pdf) | ISBN 9781071827703 (epub) | ISBN 9781071827697 (epub)

Subjects: LCSH: Social justice and education. | Social justice–Study and teaching–United States. | Anti-racism–Study and teaching–United States. | Critical race theory–United States. | Educational equalization–United States. | Critical pedagogy–United States. | Teachers–Training of–United States.

Classification: LCC LC192.2 .B45 2024 | DDC 379.2/60973–dc23/eng/20231117

LC record available at https://lccn.loc.gov/2023049312

This book is printed on acid-free paper.

23 24 25 26 27 10 9 8 7 6 5 4 3 2 1

Contents

Companion
Website Contents

 Visit the companion website at
https://resources.corwin.com/RadicalLove
for the following downloadable resources:

Figure 2.2: Note Taking Graphic Organizer

Figure 3.3: Equity Action Plan Overview

Figure 3.4: Identity Map (Blank Version)

Chapter 6: Social Justice Educator Checklist

Acknowledgments

There are many people I have to thank for having arrived at this point in my life. First of all, God is my source and without God I would not be writing these words or in a position to be heard. Thank you God for the gift of writing, which I discovered at the age of 9. I have always wanted to write a book and through this journey, many days felt too long or too short. You kept me sane and you kept me going. Amen. I want to thank all of my teachers growing up in Brooklyn, New York, particularly the difficult ones who did not believe in me as a young Black girl in a gifted education program. Many thought I was too loud and too sure of myself. Well, here I am, still loud and still certain that I was meant to be a writer. Thank you for starting an unshakeable fire in me to change education from the inside out, starting with myself, of course.

To my editors, Lucas and Dan. From the beginning, you valued my work and guided me along this journey from start to finish. Thank you for all of the edits, the conversations, the radical honesty among us when we had different philosophies but the same goal, to get this book out into the world. I am forever grateful that we met at AERA back in 2019.

To my dear friend Eve Eure, who I met in graduate school at Teachers College, Columbia University. You are one of the few I can trust to tell me the truth, to lift me up and to keep me grounded in the face of deep adversity and tribulations. I am glad we made it through many storms together and became stronger as sistafriends. Thank you for believing in my work and for supporting me.

To my sistafriend Leniece! Thank you for always telling me I am enough and that you believe in the power of my work to change the world. I sent many videos explaining this work to you repeatedly and you never got tired of me.

Thank you to the greatest teacher I have ever had, Dr. Emily J. Klein. I met you in ninth grade and it was the beginning of a beautiful friendship that has spanned decades, places and spaces. You have inspired me since day one and continue to do so. Thanks for always speaking words of affirmation into me in the form of texts, FB messages, and listening to my very random voice notes. I love you.

To my birthday twin and wonderful friend Dr. Katie O'Grady. Your friendship has brought so much joy and radical love into my life. Thank you for seeing me and being there for me during some of the most difficult seasons in my life, which occurred while writing this book.

To my incredible research participants, thank you for your time, energy, and patience with this process. Thank you for trusting me to share your story and for believing in my vision for this book. I appreciate each of you.

To my mom, Jackie Belle, for bringing me into this world and for giving me timeless swag and Black woman magic. I love you. To my brother, Jarmil Belle, for always listening to my complaints, my highs, and my lows as I struggled to write this book. You always answer the phone on the first ring. You are always there through it all and I do not take that for granted.

And last, but certainly not least, to my INCREDIBLE children, who love me unconditionally, who believe in me and who are my biggest supporters. Thank you for having patience with me when I wrote during weekends and often late into the night after bedtime. Zena, Kenzo, and Zora, you are the reason, always and forever.

PUBLISHER'S ACKNOWLEDGMENTS

Corwin gratefully acknowledges the contributions of the following reviewers:

Neil MacNeill
Educational mentor, teacher, and writer
Ellenbrook Primary School
Perth, Western Australia

Renee Ponce-Nealon
Teacher
Petaluma City Schools
Petaluma, California

Catherine Sosnowski
Adjunct Professor
Central Connecticut State University
New Britain, Connecticut

About the Author

Dr. Crystal Belle has been an educator for over 17 years and has worked in k-12 schools in Brooklyn, New York, as an English Teacher, in higher education at the University of Houston-Downtown and Rutgers University-Newark as a Professor and Director of Education, and in the nonprofit sector as a Director of curriculum partnerships at EL Education. Her work is grounded in Critical Race Theory (CRT), Social Justice Education, radical love, and self-care. Also an entrepreneur, Dr. Belle is the founder and Principal consultant of Self Love Life 101, an online coaching business that supports individuals and organizations to implement radical self-care through Diversity, Equity, and Inclusion frameworks in order to achieve their goals. Currently, Dr. Belle is the Diversity, Equity, and Inclusion Manager (North America) at Ralph Lauren. Also a poet, Belle is the author of *Woman on Fire*, a poetry collection that explores Black womanhood through race, class, and education. Her writing has been featured in *Journal of Black Studies*, *Journal of Adolescent and Adult Literacy*, *Education Week*, *Education Review*, *The London School of Economics Blog for United States Politics and Policy*, *Includr*, and *Medium*.

Originally from Brooklyn, New York, Dr. Belle is a proud student of NYC public schools from k-12. After earning a Posse scholarship and graduating at the top of her high school class, Dr. Belle went on to complete her undergraduate studies at Middlebury College with a Bachelor's Degree in English Literature (*cum laude*). She eventually continued her education and earned Master's Degrees in Education from Pace University and Teachers College of Columbia University. Dr. Belle received her doctorate in English Education from Teachers College of Columbia University and received the Teachers College dissertation fellowship to complete her study that focused on Black masculinities in NYC public schools and used portraiture, poetry, and CRT as a research method.

Last but certainly not least, Dr. Belle is a loving mother of three children and loves spending time with her family. She also loves knitting, crocheting, sewing, and resting on the couch with her cat. When she is not mothering, loving, writing, or working, you can find her on Instagram/Facebook/X: @selflovelife101.

Introduction: This Is No Ordinary Love

B ecause the word is overused and often undertheorized, I want to begin with how I define the concept of love, and specifically, the concept of radical love. Love, in the context of education, continues to be misunderstood and underused as a powerful tool for social justice. But what exactly is social justice education? This book serves as a radical and loving testimony to continuously answer this question throughout the peaks and valleys of every chapter. This book targets those who teach in K-12 classrooms, administrators, and leaders who work directly with teachers, directors of higher education teacher certification programs (secondary/elementary) as well as education consultants working with schools and districts to implement social justice teaching and learning methods.

The concept of love in education is not a novel idea. I wonder though, if there was ever a time when love was unique. Maybe when the world began? That question is directly connected to one's ideological beliefs, or perhaps one's religion. Can you imagine someone discovering love for the first time? Many tend to understand this feeling personally, in the sense of romantic love. But I want us to understand that we are *born* into love. I do not want to assume that I know or understand the hearts of all those who bring life into the world: biological parents, surrogate mothers, and adoptive parents; their experiences are all different in important ways. As a mother, I know there is an unimaginable amount of love that goes into carrying, birthing, and raising children.

Some experiences are certainly more privileged than others, some less. Once a child leaves the womb and enters the world, what happens to them depends on the parents, guardians, and caretakers that await them, and on the world, they encounter through institutions, organizations, and the outdoors.

Those who are not biological parents share in various aspects of parental love too, as aunts or uncles, godparents, baby-sitters, friends, and neighbors. There are many ways to show deep love for others, and it is often assumed to be a more "serious" matter when bloodlines are at stake. But we know that, although our understanding of love tends to be confined to familial and romantic notions, love is in fact universal, and it exists outside of these relationships. I want to discuss this love that exists within us, and that cannot exist without us. Love needs us and we need love.

To be educated can mean many things. In the most basic terms, to be educated is to be taught or to learn something, either by oneself or with others. Therefore, to teach is an act of love, or it should be, as it facilitates the acquisition of knowledge through a relationship of care. Sharing information that can improve someone's life in some way, shape, or form is powerful. Exposing someone to information they were not privy to before can lead to an exchange of ideas, which leads to an expansion of the mind, and critical thinking.

But what if the knowledge shared is dangerous and harmful to the group of people learning it because it ignores their lived experiences? Is this kind of teaching still an act of love? Surely, it is not. This is why teaching as an intentional act of love is something all teachers should be prepared for; knowing what is and isn't harmful isn't always easy or intuitive. In an ever-changing and highly diverse society that encompasses a rich array of races, ethnicities, cultures, languages, and sexual and gender identities as well as a range of abilities, teaching with love must be understood as an intersectional process.

There are students all over the nation—rural and urban, rich, and poor—who are being taught in classrooms that need clearer and more direct evidence of love. This love cannot be witnessed in the structures of term papers or the occasional handshake before entering the classroom. This love must be made so visible that it is an actual feeling of clear and present safety upon walking into the school building and its classrooms. This love looks and sounds like vulnerability among teachers and students. This love looks like students making mistakes and receiving the affirmation they need to try again. This love looks like understanding **who** a student is outside of standardized test scores and grade point averages. This is no ordinary love. It is *radical* love from the depths of the heart. As explored in the book *Street Data: A Next-Generation Model for Equity, Pedagogy and School Transformation*, the love I am describing is also reflective of a "vision of what is possible when we build classrooms and schools and systems around students' brilliance, cultural wealth, cultural wealth and intellectual potential, rather than self-serving savior narratives that have us 'fixing' and 'filling' academic gaps" (Safir & Dugan, 2021, p. 4).

To help visualize this love, let us think about chakras. In yoga and meditation, chakras refer to how energy moves through the body. The various emotional, physical, and spiritual energies of teachers and students inside and outside of the classroom impact how they interact with one another daily. Of the seven main chakras, the fourth is the heart chakra, located at the center of your chest. This chakra is said to impact your ability to love while under-standing and accepting people for who they are. When I imagine the kind of love capable of transforming and uplifting a classroom space, it is fourth-chakra love: the ability to both heal and inspire others due to a deeper understanding of oneself and one's purpose in the world. This healing love is what helps distinguish personal/familial love and radical love. To teach with a fourth chakra love is to teach with a radical desire to understand and to heal oneself through one of the most radical acts of compassion: teaching (Figure 1).

FIGURE 1 ● The Heart Chakra, Also Called *Anahata*, Is Located in the Center of the Chest and Is Associated With Openness and Cooperation

Source: iStock.com/Ramziya Abdrakhmanova

The heart chakra controls our ability to create stable bridges between our world and the worlds of others. These bridges are in the form of various relationships throughout the course of our lives: friendships, partnerships, book clubs, organizational memberships, etc. To nurture and sustain the health of these relationships, we must have an open heart. Our hearts represent the space where we allow compassion to lead instead of the ego. By "the worlds of others," I mean the physical spaces people inhabit as well as the experiences, ideas, actions, and knowledge we obtain when interacting with people. The more bridges we build, the more our heart chakra opens to the possibility of deeper forms of compassion and love. The deeper our compassion and love, the better our teaching.

I have learned, however, that due to various levels of preparation in the teaching profession (which includes traditional and alternative routes to certification), many teachers are underprepared to teach in a way that is humanizing, compassionate, and loving for both them and their students. Additionally, culturally responsive teacher preparation programs that are centered on social justice teaching and learning frameworks are not the norm nationwide. As a result, what should be a noble act (teaching) often becomes a performative dance among state mandates, overzealous testing companies more interested in profit than student learning (Strauss, 2015), and oppressive pedagogical practices.

Understanding your motivation for teaching (and what that entails in the 21st century) is, therefore, crucial for creating spaces of love and healing in schools and the communities that surround them. We must desire more, and better, than what is mandated. When we intentionally create pedagogical spaces that are holistic, healing, and anti-oppressive, we are taking part in a radical act because it is outside of the typical ways of teaching and learning that focus on data more than the minds, bodies, and souls of how students, teachers, leaders, and staff engage in the daily processes of schooling. Our understanding of data itself must expand to include "...students' homes, in the hallways, in virtual meetings, in phone calls, and in the micro-interactions among teachers and students" (Safir & Dugan, 2021, p. 4). An expansion of how we see and understand student progress is a critical component of social justice teaching and learning methods.

Love is the beginning of this conversation. To go deeper, radical love is the critical fourth-chakra extension, which strengthens from the root. Think of a beautiful tree covered in flowers. Its leaves and blooms are probably the first thing you notice, but it is the soil and the roots that support its growth and existence. Let us think about this image in the context of schools. Do teachers and schools operate in service of deep, healthy roots? Or do they operate as if only fruit and flowers matter? Based on my lived experiences as a teacher, consultant, professor, and educational researcher, many schools throughout the nation operate in service of only one or the other. Some will care deeply for their students but fail to prepare them for state-mandated tests. Others will excel with high test scores but neglect their students' identities. Creating a social justice education grounded in radical love requires caring for the root, trunk, and branches, seamlessly strengthening all aspects of education in a more enlightened, loving, and healing way. Schools need to be mini replicas of the strongest trees around us, providing security, shade, oxygen, food, and lasting love that can withstand the storms that always come.

I began this introduction by writing about birth and love due to the biases and perspectives that I have as a Black mother in a world that despises Black people. To birth a child is to literally bring new life into the world. This act, often used metaphorically in creative ventures, implies the creation of something *new*, something we *do not yet understand*, something we *aspire to*, or something we have reimagined or re-envisioned. Yet, because of where they live, their class status, the status of their parents, and the kinds of healthcare or food they have access to, many children are placed into predetermined boxes upon birth. Therefore, even the act of birthing, literal or figurative, is subject to liberating and oppressive forces, depending on your race, class, gender, ability, and sexuality.

As I write these words, the impact of the coronavirus has had a disproportionate effect on Black people nationwide due to the impact of racism and inequities of all kinds, from the economic to the geopolitical. This was true at the beginning of the pandemic, and it remains true now, three years later. George Floyd in Minnesota, Breonna Taylor in Kentucky, Ahmaud Arbery in Georgia, and Maurice Gordon here in my home state of New Jersey were all murdered at the hands of police. It would be easy for me, living in a Black body, with Black children and a Black partner, in a world that seemingly hates Black people, to reject the notion of radical love, to turn away from my fourth chakra.

But I chose to give birth to this book instead. I stand on the shoulders of great scholars before me, like Toni Morrison, James Baldwin, and Audre Lorde. I also stand in solidarity with current scholars who are pushing the field of education: Eve Ewing, Shawn Ginwright, and Yolanda Sealey Ruiz, to name a few. As I give birth to a text rooted in the traditions of social justice and Critical Race Theory (CRT), I invite you into my delivery room, where there are no machines, intravenous contraptions, or drugs. In this delivery room, you will laugh, cry, smile, wonder, create, and grow. You will be pushed to reimagine an educational landscape that does not need to measure social justice frameworks in its schools because it is evident to every onlooker. You will be asked to admit your own shortcomings while being offered strategies to overcome them in your school, community, and family.

Start with Radical Love is a testament to love and the power of social justice to restructure oppressive educational practices and sustain new ways of teaching and learning alongside students. It uses a narrative and portraiture approach (Lawrence-Lightfoot & Davis, 1997) to unpack and uncover the nuances of teaching for justice in a nation where we still have to say "Black lives matter!" A portraiture approach is creative and is often coupled with personal narratives to blur the boundaries of research as a way to capture the complexity of the human experience (Miller, Liu, & Ball, 2020). Such an approach is aligned with the overall resistance to dehumanizing schooling practices described throughout the text along with strategies for us to do better as a collective community. This book is written for those of us who have been called to teach and to lead teachers, and for those who manage school leaders at the district level. It is important to note that this book is a radical testimony, centered in love and is an intentional disruption of traditional educational texts. This is not a curriculum guide or a handbook. This is not a pedagogical toolkit, although pedagogical activities are offered throughout the chapters as a social justice offering to restructure classrooms that operate primarily in the spaces of control and hierarchy. This book uses personal testimonies and lived experiences as a Critical Race counternarrative, which are narratives told from the perspectives of those who have been historically marginalized (Mora, 2014). These CRT counter-narratives will challenge the reader to reimagine how they perceive the act of schooling and how we can unlearn harmful ways of teaching and learning that oppress more than they inspire. The word counter implies resistance to dominant structures and ways of being/know, re: white.

In Chapter 1, we begin with an introduction to Social Justice Education (SJE) and its innate connection to radical love. In

Chapter 2, the roots of my SJE framework are broken down into theoretical and practical examples, which can be used in the classroom immediately. In Chapter 3, I introduce CRT and its connections to heart healing through teaching and learning, educator beliefs, and the structural inequities that plague our classrooms. In Chapter 4, we will apply what we have learned to Special Education and we will explore strategies for recreating inclusive classrooms that honor students with different needs. We will also explore the role of the School-to-Prison Pipeline and various policies and practices about Special Education. In Chapter 5, we will read the narratives of those who aspire to refine their craft as social justice educators on a daily basis, and we will hear their stories as they learn new strategies and implement them both inside and outside the classroom. Their narratives will be merged with my own perspectives and perceptions of their understanding of Social Justice Education. Chapter 6 concludes by emphasizing a new way of teaching and learning that is rooted in Social Justice Education, CRT, and student-centered approaches to pedagogy that embrace care, cultural curiosity, creativity, and of course, radical love.

To get the most out of this book, I want you to open your fourth chakra and feel that opening in the center of your chest. Inhale and exhale with me as we go through this journey together. As you breathe deeply, I want you to think about your own educational journey from kindergarten through high school. What worked and why? What was missing for you in school that you feel hindered your educational journey? If you have never had to think about these kinds of questions, I want you to look deeply into your heart and explore why that is the case.

Every chapter will include a radical love note that is connected to the theme of the chapter. As you read, the goal is to have you thinking pedagogically in a way that is centered on love. The radical love notes will be followed by chapter objectives to provide an overview of the structure of the chapter and its overall purpose about Social Justice Education. The chapters include a combination of pedagogical activities and some reflective prompts, primarily for educators to pause and reflect, as a way to honor self-care and our humanity. Lastly, the chapters conclude with a radical love pedagogical activity and/or tips that embody key chapter themes, along with discussion questions that you can incorporate into your classrooms and are meant to be scaffolded according to grade level.

In order to gain the most from this book, it is important to remember that this is also an ongoing radical testimony, as told from the many spaces I have had the privilege of being an educator within. There is joy, there is pain and unapologetic truth-telling from the perspective of a Critical Race Theorist (myself) as I/you/me/we sit with the knowledge that CRT is currently being banned in several schools nationwide, simply for telling the truth about the complex history of racism in the United States. The way I choose to tell this story is an intentional disruption of the status quo and traditional conceptions of academic and educational writing. I hope you are excited about the journey ahead of you, it will definitely inspire you and challenge you, simultaneously.

CHAPTER 1

What's Love Got to Do With It?

RADICAL LOVE NOTE #1

Have you ever been in a situation where you loved someone but failed to be in love with their behavior? This happens all the time in classrooms. Teachers are overwhelmed by bureaucratic paperwork, standardized testing, and low compensation. Therefore, they do not often have the time or energy to truly fall in love with their students, whatever their perceived flaws might be. Quite often, we use student behaviors as a measure of their academic aptitude, which is a clear and undeniable example of bias. It is not possible to love and challenge them to become better versions of themselves without also accepting their flaws (especially since we all have them). When we help our students become better versions of themselves, we honor who they are and the significance of their current and ongoing contributions to creating and sustaining a stronger sense of humanity nationwide, and even globally. However, as education funding continues to shrink and as unqualified government officials continue to make racist and non-research-based decisions, our most vulnerable populations (Black, Brown, Asian and Indigenous people, undocumented students, transgender students, and students with disabilities) are the individuals who are often loved the least.

What does that mean, you wonder? It means that for Black people like me, love fades quickly, even when we make up the majority of urban cities and school districts (where property tax dollars are not as expensive as in wealthier suburban areas). As a result, these students are often seen as burdens before they are given a chance to become who they are meant to be: the best versions of themselves.

Regarding class, low-income white folks in communities nationwide also suffer from economic oppression due to the traumatic impact of low-income housing and limited educational resources and opportunities. Conversely, wealthy white students living and going to schools in affluent communities are frequently (and automatically) presumed to be intellectuals, primarily because assumptions are made that equate generational wealth and privilege, the key components of a privileged American (white) lifestyle, with intelligence and success. I am speaking of and about seemingly different groups of people in the same love note because my first affirmation of love to you is this: intersectionality and inclusivity are the foundation of a radical love framework.

Chapter Objective

In this chapter, as we begin to answer the question of what social justice education (SJE) is, we will examine privilege, specifically how it shows up in our respective lives depending on our race/ethnicity, gender, class, and ability. It is important to note that privilege, who has access to it, and how it is leveraged, specifically when it comes to power structures inside and outside of school walls, is an ongoing theme throughout the book. Through a deep examination of privilege, the chapter will explore conceptions of "urban" and how it impacts the ways teachers see and understand themselves in relation to their students on a daily basis. Through these larger themes of privilege and unpacking the meaning of urban, there are specific tools that are both pedagogical as well as self-care based, that will serve as opportunities to think about intentional strategies to shift oppressive and harmful teaching practices that are inequitable for students. The tools are guided by my SJE framework pillars (which lay the basics of the framework outlined in the following chapter) that guide reflection prompt activities for teachers to think about. This serves as a way to center self-reflection from a space of our collective humanity and radical love. Every chapter ends with a radical love activity and debrief which is specifically meant to create more inclusive and humanizing learning activities for students. These activities are mostly general and easy to follow, with a focus on literacy, language, and love and should be scaffolded accordingly, depending on the grade level you teach. **It is important to note that the reflection prompt activities are geared toward Professional Learning Communities (PLCs)**

(Continued)

(Continued)

whereas the Radical Love Activities are centered on student-driven pedagogy and designed to take place in a classroom setting to disrupt the typical classroom flow as a way to honor social justice teaching and learning practices.

PRIVILEGE AND IMAGINATION: WHAT DO WE BRING TO OUR CLASSROOMS?

A young, petite, white woman with a short black pixie cut, light green eyes, and a slight smile on her face entered my 21st Century Urban Education course on the first day of class. It was the Spring semester, although outside it still looked like winter thanks to New Jersey snowstorms in 2018. I saw her immediately because she was one of the first people to enter the stuffy white and red room where I taught. As a result, my plans for having a quiet, meditative moment before the students arrived were suddenly relinquished. My desire to meditate and ground myself in the space before students enter the classroom is one of the ways I embody who I fully am while teaching. I don't want to be too vulnerable in front of my students, so when this opportunity to meditate escapes me, I tend to find another way to enter that space.

In this case, I looked directly at the woman (named Hannah) and said: "Good afternoon, welcome to 21st Century Urban Education!" To be honest, my words did not yet match my mood, but my intention was to get to that level within the next 20 minutes when the class would officially start. Hannah returned the greeting and sat upright in her seat, seemingly eager to begin.

Twenty minutes later, the class was packed with both young and middle-aged preservice teachers, which was a benefit of teaching at this institution. We had a wide range of students that varied in age, socioeconomic background, race, and ability. It is one of the reasons I loved working there, as it reminded me of the beauty and necessity of having folks from diverse backgrounds engage with one another in the classroom, and hopefully push one another to be the best versions of themselves. On the first day of class, I did what many instructors, professors, and teachers do; I explained the goals of the course and the syllabus to ensure that everyone was on the same page.

During that time, I allowed students to ask clarifying questions before moving on to the icebreaker activities. The icebreaker I chose for the first day of class was "What is your understanding of the word 'urban'?" I ask this question because of the nature of the course and program, which are both centered in Urban Education. Students having deep misconceptions of the word "urban," often equating it with "deficit" or "inferior," was a struggle I constantly faced in the classroom. As such, I had future teachers unpack their understanding of the word to get to the root of why they wanted to become urban educators in the first place. As the students began to discuss their conceptions, the typical negative answers arose: poor, dilapidated, hopeless, and utter despair. As I listened to their words, I prepared myself emotionally and mentally to allow them to share fully and freely. I understood that I had a responsibility to push them on their deficit conceptions of urban environments, which meant I needed to know what they were first.

In the article "Imagining the Urban: The Politics of Race, Class and Schooling," Zeus Leonardo and Margaret Hunter discuss how most conceptions of the word urban are "imagined" (Leonardo & Hunter, 2007). In other words, many are socialized into believing that "urban" is bad and "suburban" is good without having substantial experiences in either environment. This allows them to recreate continuous and hopeless scenarios in their minds when it comes to understanding what it means for a place to be urban, and by extension what it means for someone to live in such a place. Think, for instance, about what you've heard about the Upper East Side of New York City versus what you have heard about south-central Los Angeles or the contradictions in how Manhattan is sometimes described versus Chicago's southside. All urban locations, all with very different reputations in the media and the popular imagination. As such, many teachers operate from spaces of stereotypical notions of urban communities and schools. According to the authors, "the urban is socially and discursively constructed as a place, which is part of the dialectical creation of the urban as both a real and imagined space. The urban, is real, insofar as it is demarcated by zones, neighborhoods, and policies. However, it is imagined to the extent that it is replete with meaning, much of which contains contradictions as to exactly what the urban signifies" (p. 779). These negative tropes attached to "urban" permeated the air in my courses on day one and throughout the semester.

I helped students start the process of unlearning these stereotypes by pushing them to think of their own identities in relation to urban schooling. While the students discussed various definitions of urban among themselves, we simultaneously moved into a discussion about privilege. I discuss white privilege, specifically in educational contexts, and the role of white teachers in classrooms to facilitate their acknowledgment of that privilege while also advocating for others who have fewer privileges. This is one way of leveling the playing field from an equity standpoint.

Hannah raised her hand at this point and, with a warm smile, I replied, "Yes, would you like to share something?" Hannah contended that, although she was white, she did not have any privilege because she lived in the Ironbound section of Newark and did not come from wealth. It's important to know that Newark is the largest city in New Jersey and considered the most "racially diverse," which is a fancy way of describing a very Black city. However, the Ironbound section of Newark identifies as predominantly white and Hispanic/Latinx, which is reflected demographically in the housing, healthcare, and schools on that side of town. Because the Ironbound sits near the city center of Newark, schools, and other social services also have more financial resources in comparison to other parts of the city. Therefore, Hannah actually lived in one of the most privileged communities in Newark, which she did not appear to consider in her declaration that her proximity to privilege was limited.

Hannah's assertion that she didn't benefit from white privilege because she lived in a predominantly Black and, in some cases, poor city, speaks to the misconceptions many future teachers have about their identities in relation to urban education and urban environments. As I listened to Hannah, I understood that it was her lack of knowledge that led her to make this bold statement as a white woman. However, I also understood that it was important to help her recognize the privilege she clearly had. Hannah continued, "When I go to other areas of New Jersey like Short Hills and they see that my driver's license has a Newark address, I am treated differently." I nodded in agreement with her slowly, like a robot attempting to avoid an argument, because I have had this same conversation too many times before with other white people who equated being poor with an automatic cancellation of the racial privileges they have because they are white.

I thought carefully about what I would say next, as I have learned that teachers have a significant role in facilitating these discussions in open and productive ways. I replied, "Hannah, I hear what you are saying and I respect your point. You are talking more about class than race, and that's good because our identities are intersectional. As such, it's important to consider the ways that race, class, and gender work in order to reinforce power and privilege, especially as a white woman." I smiled gently, wanting Hannah to know that I was not dismissing her point, but pushing her to think about the ways that her privileges as a white woman exist.

I could see her become uncomfortable. She swayed gently in her seat as though she was ready to leave the room. I was not surprised, as I have become immune to these kinds of responses from white students who feel safer denying their privilege rather than accepting how they can use their privilege to become powerful social justice educators. She finally replied, this time with anger in her voice, "You do not know me! I do not have privileges. My family does not have a lot of money and I know what it means to struggle. I am not privileged at all!" The class becomes silent.

Everyone, including me, stared back at Hannah, trying to figure out where we should take the conversation.

I begin this chapter with Hannah's story not to center her white woman fragility or privilege but rather to point out the complex nature of teaching future teachers. It must inherently start with love before the hard work of unpacking one's biases can actually begin. Radical love is a critical tenet of an SJE framework. We cannot teach those we do not love and students cannot learn deeply from others who they feel do not love them. Considering the notion that there is always "a place for love in any movement for social justice" (hooks, 2000, p. xix), instead of responding to Hannah with anger and frustration, I responded with love, because as a teacher educator, I must have the ability to see the good in every future teacher. Even though Hannah was not ready to receive the reality of her racial privilege in the world, at least she was encouraged to think about it and unpack it in a safe and supportive space.

REFLECTION PROMPT ACTIVITY FOR TEACHERS

The purpose of this reflection prompt is to think about how race plays a role in our daily interactions, personally and professionally. Writing helps to release some of our deepest thoughts while encouraging us to think of strategies that create more socially just and loving classrooms. More importantly, we cannot discuss social justice without addressing how race plays a role in how we see and under-stand the world.

Prompt #1: If you are Black, Brown, Latinx, Indigenous, Native American, or Asian, how does it feel when you are in a room where the majority of people are of color? How does it feel when the majority of people are of your same racial/ethnic background? How does it feel when the majority of people are white?

Prompt #2: If you are white or white presenting, how does it feel when you are in a room where the majority of people are of color? How does it feel when the majority of people are white?

Take 10–15 minutes in order to reflect on these writing prompts. As you write, consider your positionality as a teacher/leader in your school. Do you represent the majority of the students? If so, how does your privilege show up in your classroom and in your interactions with students and staff? Do you represent a minority of students? If so, how does that make you feel? Is this lack of diverse representation also reflected in the leadership of staff at your school? [All responses should be kept in a shared drive folder that everyone who participates has access to. The goal is to use their responses as a way to advocate for and explore social-justice-minded teacher reflections and self-awareness].

Note: This activity is specifically designed for PLCs and Professional Development working sessions.

When you finish the writing activity, share it in your group and discuss your feelings. You may become emotional during this activity, as it may activate strong feelings in your heart. The goal is to deepen our understanding of one another as colleagues and as social justice educators. After everyone shares their reflection, come up with a strategy for moving forward. As a group, come up with a working list of at least five professional behaviors the group can adopt to create more antiracist teaching and learning spaces through deep reflection and radical love.

In Glenn Singleton's third edition of *Courageous Conversations About Race* (2021) he notes that "in schools, as well as in other agencies and institutions, race plays a primary role in sustaining if not widening the omnipresent achievement gaps."

"But educators, as well as corporate and community leaders, have not been willing to enter into discussion about this extraordinarily complex and emotionally charged topic" (p. 7). Ignoring the impact of racism in our schools only perpetuates oppressive teaching and learning practices that maintain stereotypical conceptions of our most vulnerable students who happen to be primarily Black and Brown. Creating intentional spaces within PLCs to explore our respective privileges based on positionality in a capitalist society, can be both healing and action-oriented. Such intentional professional learning opportunities can encourage us to take the steps to create a more inclusive and racially just world through teaching and learning.

RADICAL LOVE AS A TOOL FOR EDUCATORS

The construction of whiteness affords one many privileges; whether one chooses to acknowledge these privileges or not, is a different story. We (white folks especially, due to proximity to privilege), must intentionally leverage our privileges through collective activism with historically marginalized communities while creating more inclusive classrooms through self-education and self-care. This comes at the risk of disrupting the status quo, a systemic machine that thrives upon racism and white supremacy. If we are all committed to this critical disruption of the status quo, we can help many of our students achieve liberation in the classroom which can impact their respective *home* communities as well.

If we are all committed to this critical disruption of the status quo, we can help many of our students achieve liberation in the classroom which can impact their respective **home** *communities as well.*

With that in mind, it's important to point out that Hannah was one of the few white people in the room. Unlike many teacher education programs, the majority of the students in this program were of color, which was a new experience for me. The diversity in the room, as well as my own Blackness, made the space new and unfamiliar for Hannah, too. I finally chimed in: "I know this is a difficult conversation, especially on the first day of class, however, here in the Urban Teacher Education Program, we are preparing social justice educators. Therefore, it is important for all of us in the room to understand the privileges we bring to the classroom. Understanding our privileges will make us more aware of how they function in our everyday lives, and clarify observations we make about other people and places. This is especially true for future educators." With that last point, I moved on with the rest of my lesson, which included building a culture of community in the course itself. Hannah was just one of many students who saw themselves as separated from the privileges they so clearly had.

Reflecting upon my argument that love is the main ingredient for teaching and learning spaces, it is important to note how radical love will be used throughout the book as a tool for teaching and learning. The very concept of being radical requires one to step outside of the boxes that have been carefully constructed for them. Many schools operate under structures of fear and dominance to maintain order and hierarchy. In scholar R. Michael Fisher's article "Radical Love: Is It Radical Enough" he argues, "In any oppressive society, the goal of the educator ought to be to look in-depth (outer and inner), while guiding others likewise through dialogue, to inquire critically below the constructive normative surfaces of existence and be willing to enter into the fear/terror (e.g., taboos) by which oppressive societies sustain their structures" (Fisher, 2017, p. 262). Because urban students often see schools as sites of trauma (i.e., sites of fear, terror, and taboos) as opposed to sites of hope and learning, it is the goal of the educator to help students unlearn trauma by fostering a critical dialogue that allows them to critique the very institutions they have been socialized to trust blindly. Assuming automatic trust without building relationships stems from hegemonic structures of fear and control, a pervasive theme in urban schools.

Similarly, in private, rural, and independent schools, although in a completely different context, there is still the belief that students must view teachers as masters of their destiny due to the power they wield in providing grades, writing letters of recommendation, and connecting students with other key networking players during their educational journey. Some research studies continue to show that teachers in independent schools, particularly those of affluence, encounter difficult relationships with parents who use their money, power, and privilege as a way of attempting to dominate the relationship with teachers, to ensure a certain level of success for their child. This too, is a cycle of control between students, teachers, and families. However, students from wealthier backgrounds may have the resources and the time to overcome these obstacles in a quicker fashion, as opposed to students from urban backgrounds who typically do not have access to as many resources and social capital.

But why am I naming every kind of student and school in this chapter? I have seen how ongoing conversations in the field of education have become polarized to the point of misunderstanding, leading to overly trite (mis)understandings of urban and suburban students, as well as private and independent students. Every school can operate in more social justice-oriented ways by adopting a radical love teaching agenda. A radical love teaching agenda incorporates four pillars from a SJE framework (Figure 1.1):

FIGURE 1.1 ● Social Justice Education Framework Pillars

(1) Understand the needs of your students on a cultural, socioeconomic, and racial level.
(2) Use the privileges you have as a teacher to leverage the playing field for students to effectively see themselves in the classroom as well as within the communities they identify with.
(3) Allow yourself to be vulnerable in front of your students to openly share your biases, while actively creating new pedagogical strategies that place student academic, emotional, and social needs at the center.
(4) Carefully construct an antiracist curriculum that infuses intersectional yet rigorous academic standards that honor the cultural capital represented by the students.

It is important to understand how each of the four pillars works within a SJE framework and how to respond to scenarios that may occur in classrooms and schools. In the following section, we will look briefly at each one and outline how they can be brought into the classroom.

THE FOUR PILLARS OF THE SOCIAL JUSTICE EDUCATION FRAMEWORK

Understand the Needs of Your Students on a Cultural, Socioeconomic, and Racial Level

Students enter our classrooms with several layers of cultural, social, economic, and racial differences. It is imperative that we are mindful of our own cultural lenses and our ways of knowing and being in the classroom. We must understand how this impacts the way we teach and respond to student learning goals. To foster such understanding, here are some key questions to ask yourself every time you enter the classroom:

1. What are my understandings of teaching and learning and how do my cultural, social, economic, and racial ways of knowing impact these understandings?

2. How can I meet students where they are at without compromising academic rigor?

3. In what ways can my classroom space become loving, humanizing, and racially literate?

Having these essential questions at the forefront of our everyday teacher readiness brains will keep us continuously aware of our students' diverse and ever-changing needs. These essential questions can also be placed somewhere in the classroom so that it is always visible, reminding students that their best interests are always top of mind.

Classroom Context: To explicitly merge theory and practice, having these questions on a poster that can be seen by all in the classroom sends a powerful message to your students. These questions can be shared as essential questions at the beginning of the year that honor teacher vulnerability and radical love. To make this activity beneficial for building relational trust in the classroom, turn each question into a statement that students can rate. On a quarterly basis (every 2–3 months) students should be provided with an anonymous survey asking them to rate the teacher on a scale from 1 to 5 for each question-turned-statement, with 1 being **least likely** and 5 being **most likely**. The results from this survey should be shared with students for transparency. Results will help students feel valued by the teacher and should drive the teacher to continuously make iterative changes, depending on students' responses and ongoing pedagogical and social-emotional needs.

Use the Privileges You Have as a Teacher to Leverage the Playing Field for Students to Effectively See Themselves in the Classroom, as Well as Within the Communities They Identify With

As a teacher, you are in a position of power, which requires you to exercise both caution and critical judgment to ensure humanizing spaces for your students. Part of truly seeing our students in the classroom is connected to the curriculum we use on a daily basis. A social justice-based curriculum centers students' lives and lived experiences. Although these pedagogical actions appear to be relatively simple, it is no secret that most classrooms nationwide are bombarded by test preparation, large classroom sizes, and a one-size-fits-all approach to student needs. To shift this industrial education design driven by intense labor and production of "goods" (educational products we force students to produce), we must get to know our students on a *real* level so that we can respond to their genuine needs. Some easy pedagogical strategies for getting to know our students are:

1. Personalized surveys asking them about their interests, learning styles, and wishes for the academic year.

2. Recurrent team-building activities in the classroom that continuously reestablish and maintain trust and community.

3. Giving students quarterly teacher evaluations that give them the space to be critical of their own teaching so you can immediately incorporate curricular changes that center their needs.

Engaging students in social justice in the 21st century requires us to be humble, yet forward-thinking considering that we live in a digital and highly technological age. The good news is that we now have multiple ways to engage students and learn more about them. The bad news is that high-stakes testing and oppressive teaching environments make it difficult for teachers to truly make the time and space to connect with their students. However, the purpose of this book is to remind you that you can still resist. The first acts of resistance as a teacher must start with loving our students deeply enough to give them what they deserve academically, emotionally, and socially.

Allow Yourself to Be Vulnerable in Front of Your Students as a Way to Openly Share Your Biases, While Actively Creating New Pedagogical Strategies That Place Students' Academic, Emotional, and Social Needs at the Center

The idea that we can remain neutral toward our students is anti-loving in nature. To love means to be vulnerable, stepping outside of ourselves in order to create a deep level of trust and understanding between ourselves and others. We do this naturally with family, partners, and friends. But what does this look like in the classroom? Loving your students means that you are interested in their academic development while simultaneously acknowledging and affirming their various identities and experiences inside and outside of the classroom. As such, structuring a curriculum to reveal student/teacher biases is a starting point for having critical dialogue in schools that can transform oppressive mindsets and habits.

The activities throughout each chapter in this book will assist you with recreating these activities in your own classrooms. I use several curricular tools to explore various forms of bias including movement, theater, novels, news articles, podcasts, Facebook posts, Instagram photos, and X campaigns, among others. The goal of using both traditional texts and popular social media platforms is to acknowledge that students are living in a highly technological society while many are still sitting in classrooms that are not up to 21st-century standards. That is a hard place to be in as a student, and it is imperative for teachers to start from a place of love and best intentions. Some clear strategies for being more vulnerable in front of your students include:

1. Share aspects of your identity with your students (where you grew up and why you chose teaching, etc.). This will deepen the bond between you and your students.

2. Create opportunities for students to share their personal stories related to their various communities and cultures. Integrating this into the curriculum will help students feel valued by you.

3. Admit when you are wrong or when you have made a mistake. Letting students know that you make mistakes is a helpful way for them to become more honest with themselves and others. You will also grow as a teacher and leader through radical honesty and love.

Carefully Construct Antiracist Curriculum That Infuses Intersectional Yet Rigorous Academic Standards That Honor the Cultural Capital Represented by the Students

I consult with and develop teachers. As a result, I hear these questions often: "Where do I start? My school gave me a scripted curriculum, what should I do?" I understand how scary it can be to develop your own curriculum, but the good news is you do not have to reinvent the wheel. There are many pre-existing resources to help you on your way to becoming a social justice educator. Some of these resources specific to a SJE framework, are listed below:

1. **National Equity Project:** An education reform organization committed to training leaders to change systems from the inside out to create more equitable and liberatory environments. Using a coaching and consulting framework, the organization works with schools, districts, and non-profits focused on educational equity work (https://www.nationalequityproject.org/).

2. **BELE (Building Equitable Learning Environments) Network:** Works with educators, policymakers, and schools to create learning environments that are student-centered and based on the science of learning research. One of the key aspects of these equitable learning environments is creating spaces where students feel valued as individuals (https://belenetwork.org/).

3. **Learning for Justice:** Originally Teaching for Tolerance, this organization provides free educational resources in the form of articles, lessons, and social justice frameworks to create shared learning opportunities among students, teachers, and school leaders. The goal of learning for justice is to uphold the mission of the Southern Poverty Law Center (https://www.splcenter.org/): to "be a catalyst for racial justice by working with communities to dismantle white supremacy, strengthen intersectional movements and advance the human rights of all people." (https://www.learningforjustice.org/)

4. **Why Social Justice in School Matters:** This article features five educators who practice social justice teaching and

learning practices through their respective activism and commitment inside and outside of the classroom. Snapshots of the way they model being social justice educators can inspire other teachers and school leaders to make changes in order to make students feel a deeper sense of belonging and psychological safety (https://www.nea.org/advocating-for-change/new-from-nea/why-social-justice-school-matters).

5. **What is Social Justice Education?** In this article featured in *Education Week* (2019), I provide an overview of SJE by offering a working definition and a framework to create a more humanizing, welcoming, and intellectual learning environment in your classroom across grade levels and content areas. There are five key tips shared to start your SJE journey (https://www.edweek.org/teaching-learning/opinion-what-is-social-justice-education-anyway/2019/01).

Radical love is a journey of cultural, emotional, personal, professional, and spiritual highs and lows that are meant to sharpen individuals to become the best versions of themselves. When we open ourselves to love and being loved, we are vulnerable and ready to receive information and endure experiences that may be outside of our comfort zones.

Similarly, a social justice educator is someone who starts with radical love to create a new pedagogical and theoretical light for themselves, their students, and the institutions they work within. Starting at the root with love allows us to transform ourselves, our students, and our respective institutions in radical and empowering ways.

UNLEARN WHAT YOU KNOW

The SJE framework pillars are the first step to unpacking the intersectional dynamics of practicing, creating, and sustaining social justice teaching and learning practices. It is no easy task. However, with care, patience, and deep love for your students, you can easily begin to practice each of the pillars in your classroom. Once you have a clear sense of the four SJE pillars, you can begin to learn about the steps for adopting a

SJE framework on a daily and enduring basis. But remember, we are still in the infancy of this book (similar to the birthing process as discussed in the introduction), and as such, let us humble ourselves and try to *unlearn* what we already think we know. One of the primary aspects of practicing SJE is the *unlearning* process, which requires you to reflect deeply about what biases you hold, your positionality in this world, and how this directly impacts your teaching and learning practices. Without a clear and reflective *unlearning* practice, it will be impossible to incorporate the four SJE pillars into your pedagogy and praxis.

So how exactly do we *unlearn*? The first step in unlearning is the process of identifying what we think we know and why. Because we are socially conditioned to follow ideological trends and thought patterns that are typically associated with money, power, and white supremacy, it is imperative for individuals to have ample opportunities to critique these socially constructed biases. The classroom is one of the best places to explore individual and systemic biases using group role-playing activities, followed by a guided question debriefing process. An example of this is called Theater of the Oppressed (TO), a community-based education program that uses theater as a tool for justice and transformation created by Brazilian writer and drama theorist, Augusto Boal. Role-playing activities include acting out difficult conversations connected to racism and oppression while using critical thinking skills to explore questions about the theater-based activities after each scenario. I used Theater of the Oppressed during my tenure as a Director of Education and as a consultant through my coaching business Self Love Life 101 (https://www.selflovelife101.com/), to help teachers and school leaders role-play potential social justice scenarios in the classroom such as:

1. Gender bias when working with students who identify as girls and boys

2. Using racially coded language during your lessons

3. Failing to acknowledge your privilege as a teacher

4. Misusing your power to reinforce oppression in your classroom/school

Engaging in Theater of the Oppressed role-playing helped educators and school leaders have fun while reflecting upon how normalized the oppression of others has become in our educational systems. Teachers and leaders also had opportunities through debriefing and critical questions about how to move forward and make better decisions to create more socially just classrooms and schools. I want you to pause and think about everything you have learned in this chapter so far. I presented you with a love note about conceptions of radical love in education, which is the heart and soul of this book. I shared a personal anecdote with you about my own experiences in the field of education as a director, professor, and consultant in various classrooms. We also explored our shared and collective humanity, its intersectional nature, and the realities reflective of race, class, and gender. Now that we have arrived at this moment, I want to advise you that the first step to unlearning is identifying and *questioning* what you think you know and why. Keep that in mind as you move through the book in the form of radical love notes and activities connected to the chapter concepts, along with guided debriefing questions and extension activities for reinforcement of the SJE framework pillars.

RADICAL LOVE ACTIVITY #1: THE COLLECTIVE HEART

Grades K–12 (Please scaffold activities according to grade level)

Learning Objective: Everyone in the classroom space will create a heart with their physical bodies as a symbolic gesture of radical love and community building.

Radical Love Goal (RLG): To develop radical and loving communities, having a conscious understanding of the physical body and how it shows up in any space is an important reminder of our collective humanity and visible differences.

Audience:

a. This activity is for educators who have a designated homeroom or advisory period where there is structured time to focus on students' social-emotional well-being. If educators do not have this designated time, it can also be done in after-school settings.

(Continued)

(Continued)

   b. Similarly, teachers can make time to disrupt the traditional classroom flow to use this activity as a way to recenter and rebuild relational trust (highly recommended) Keep in mind that you will have to scaffold this activity according to grade level. The activity is general enough to be used for grades K–12 with appropriate modifications depending on student comprehension and academic/social-emotional needs.

   c. Last but certainly not least, PLCs can use this exercise as a Professional Development opportunity among teachers and leaders to create a stronger school culture and community over time.

Materials needed: large open space, pens, pencils, markers, paper, and tablet/laptop.

Everyone in the classroom space is responsible for forming a large heart by use of bodies only. There is no talking allowed and the group must choose four leaders to help assist smaller groups of people. Chosen leaders do not have to be teachers; it is recommended that teachers step back and let students choose their own leaders for this activity. Boundaries should be set for how the group will move around the space to ensure everyone's safety and consent.

Total Activity Time = 10 minutes.

Debrief: Upon constructing the group heart, sit down as a class and discuss how the process was for you and why. = 20 minutes. One teacher/leader will help with the debrief process by ensuring that everyone who wants to share, has an opportunity to discuss their experience using the questions provided in the Activity Debrief below.

Activity Debrief, Questions, and Summary

   a. What kinds of leaders were chosen to help manage the group?

   b. Why do you think the leaders were chosen?

   c. How did you feel doing this activity on a scale of 1–10 and why?

   d. If you had to recreate this activity, what would you change?

The purpose of the extension assignments is to reinforce what was learned over time, as a group.

   a. If the activity is in a traditional classroom setting, have students choose one of the extension activities as a project to present to the class at a later time (one week is perfect to return to the discussion).

b. For PLCs, have every participant choose an extension assignment to present at the following meeting (the following month/week), as a way to reinforce social justice ways of knowing and being.

Extension Assignments (Please Scaffold and Choose According to Grade Level)

1. Write an essay from the perspective of one of the group leaders. Why do you believe they were chosen and why? Use the first-person narrative "I" when you write from the perspective of the leader. It would be a good idea for leaders to write from the perceived perspectives of the participants and for the participants to write as the perceived voices of the leaders. In this way, the participants' voices will be reconstructed by those who were the leaders, and the leaders' voices will be reconstructed by those who were the participants. This exchange of "power" can create a dynamic conversation regarding equity and group dynamics.

2. Create a poem about equity based on the group activity. The poem should include visual reenactments of what occurred during the activity through words and/or images/drawings.

3. Draw a visual representation of the activity as you saw it. You may include comic strips, digital stories, or one standalone image/portrait (Photography is welcomed, as well). Develop an artist statement that includes the title of the portrait and what it signifies to you (a standalone drawing of what the activity represented can be used for earlier grades that are not writing yet).

Use these pedagogical activities and debriefs to elevate the larger themes in the chapter regarding the SJE pillars, our collective humanity and radical love. Depending on your school schedule, you may begin with the activity and debrief and follow up on another day with the extension activities to reinforce what was learned. If you have a longer block period, you can start with the activity and debrief as a collective group and use the extension activities as independent learning and reflection time.

Creating schooling environments guided by radical love through icebreaker activities and an ethic of care will allow us to be more honest about our identities, privileges, and access to various levels of power depending on where we sit in the world. Confronting our privileges together will center opportunities for transformative teaching and learning practices through collective healing.

CHAPTER 2

What Exactly Is Social Justice Education?

Social Justice Education envisions the full and equitable participation of people from all social identity groups in a society that is mutually shaped to meet their needs. (Bell, 2016, p. 1)

RADICAL LOVE NOTE #2

One of the most radical aspects of the human heart is that it keeps us alive every day. Without our hearts pumping blood through our bodies and helping our brains understand how we feel and experience the world, we would be unable to navigate our complex emotions. Until very recently, it was commonly believed that the relationship between the heart and the brain was unidirectional: the brain tells the heart to beat, but little information travels in the opposite direction. However, in the 1960s and 1970s, in the field of psychophysiology, researchers John and Beatrice Lacey discovered that the heart and the brain operate in a partnership, stating "that communication between the heart and brain actually is a dynamic, ongoing, two-way dialogue, with each organ continuously influencing the other's function" (Phoenix, 2019).

As I write these words, the coronavirus has dominated our lives for more than two years, which has led to many broken hearts, both physical and spiritual. Now, many hearts that beat so freely before this unexplainable disease invaded the world have stopped. In the wake of its first wave, job scarcity, Zoom school for my elementary-aged children, and financial scarcity seeped into my family deeply and fully. As a first-generation Black woman in a supposedly more privileged position than other "regular" Black folk because of my degrees (two from an Ivy League institution), I was suddenly faced with an unexpected layoff (after being furloughed throughout the summer), no severance pay, and very little time to recover as the primary breadwinner for our family of four. I had to ask myself, what does a commitment to social justice look like when the perils of capitalism stand at your front door? Of course, finite value cannot be placed upon one's ability to think and act upon these thoughts freely. In a nation where censorship is increasingly normalized due to highly conservative political leadership seeping in both white supremacy and patriarchy, using my mind for a living is an act of liberation. Now, I have transitioned to a Diversity, Equity, and Inclusion role in the corporate space, which allows me to use my skills as a scholar and thought leader to center social justice ways of knowing and being. Although my work looks different, the mission is the same: to create equitable opportunities for everyone, regardless of what they look like or where they come from. I am here, with you, writing this book, because I understand, as the great James Baldwin said, "to act is to be committed, and to be committed is to be in danger." To love social justice is to accept the dangers that come with disrupting the status quo.

Love **is** even when you are not. This means that, even when your students have yet to realize the potential locked within them, you do not get to place them into boxes with labels like "low-achieving" or "at-high-risk." Instead, you must love them through their struggles, because, as we know, to transform education into social justice education (SJE) requires deep struggle because it disrupts the status quo. To change racist systems of education through social justice requires conflict with the educational stakeholders who have much to lose: testing companies, for-profit charter schools who prioritize making a profit over the well-being of students and families, politicians, etc. What do we typically do when we are confronted with conflict? Some of us run, some of us fight on the front lines, and some of us write books like this to remind you that you are not alone. The struggle has never been solely black and white. Rather, it exists in a gray area where we have to demolish what is no longer serving us and create stronger systems grounded in love and social justice.

At this moment, I want you to pause and remember your heart. As you read this, place a hand over it, notice its rhythm, and notice how it aligns with your breathing patterns. The struggle for SJE and living a more humanizing life all around requires us to stop and listen to our hearts, to remember that we are here, alive, and have opportunities to be better.

Chapter Objective

In this chapter, you will be introduced to my SJE framework (an extension of the pillars) and why it is a critical component of teaching and learning in the 21st century. I explore the connections among SJE, Critical Race Theory (CRT), intersectionality (the idea that our identities are multifaceted), portraiture (a research methodology with various layers to be explored throughout the book), and a concept I call Radical Love Engagement (RLE), which is connected to healing and radical vulnerability to deepen relational trust, an aspect of radical love, which is a recurring theme throughout this book. The purpose of this chapter is to understand the complexities that shape and mold an SJE framework. It is not a one-size-fits-all model, rather it is an opportunity to build upon the nuances of our identities to strengthen the ways we interact with each other in the classroom, in schools, and within our respective communities. This chapter is designed to push against the status quo through intentional liberation strategies rooted in a portraiture research methodology that includes creativity, critical observation, and analysis to make sense of the spaces we occupy on a daily basis. As a result, I name oppressive teaching and learning practices that do more harm than good, while offering five key healing strategies to make your classroom more loving for your students by embracing collective radical self-care. Lastly, I end the chapter with a helpful pedagogical activity that uses visual literacy and current affairs to reimagine a more socially just world.

THE SOCIAL JUSTICE EDUCATION FRAMEWORK

Understanding the parameters of SJE is crucial to becoming and sustaining your journey as a social justice educator. The framework below is directly connected to the social justice pillars outlined in Chapter 1. Essentially, the pillars inform the framework below that undergirds this book (Figure 2.1).

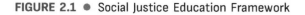

FIGURE 2.1 ● Social Justice Education Framework

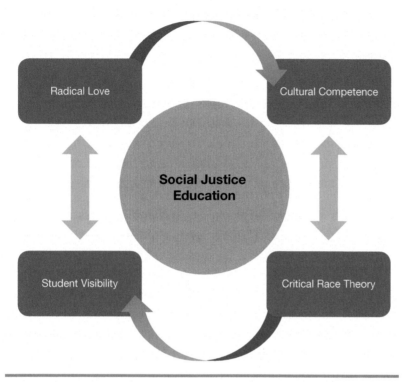

An SJE framework is intersectional in nature, with the understanding that honoring social justice teaching and learning practices is always at the center. The term "intersectionality" was first used in 1989 by American civil rights advocate and leading CRT scholar Kimberlé Crenshaw to specifically draw attention to bias and violence toward Black women. In other words, intersectionality accounts for how multiple identities are often erased depending on who has access and power. For example, if a Black woman accuses a particular organization of discrimination and the argument used against her is that they have hired other Black women, that Black woman's experience is perceived as monolithic, as opposed to completely different from another Black woman in the same organization. If one Black woman identifies as gay and disabled and another Black woman identifies as heterosexual and able-bodied, their respective experiences in that particular organization are completely different. As Crenshaw put it in a 2017 interview:

Intersectionality is a lens through which you can see where power comes and collides, where it interlocks and intersects. It's not simply that there's a race problem here, a gender problem here, and a class or LBGTQ problem there. Many times that framework erases what happens to people who are subject to all of these things. (Columbia Law School)

In other words, individuals have intersecting identities that are not solely one thing or another, but rather a complex system of multiple experiences that make up who we are. Limiting individuals to singular identities erases many aspects of who they are in order to fit into narrow boxes that reinforce the status quo.

Beyond its roots in legal theory, we can understand intersectionality as the confluence of the different parts of a person's identity, whether it be race, gender, sexual orientation, religion, class, ethnicity, ability, or age, especially as those parts relate to social inequalities (Collins, 2015). With respect to the SJE framework, acknowledging intersectionality means acknowledging the entirety of your students' identities. As shown in the model above, a praxis centered on social justice starts with radical love, which honors, respects, and protects students' right to feel authentically free in the classroom. Authentic freedom in an SJE context requires that your students feel safe enough to be their full selves and that they are not punished for being who they are.

Authentic freedom in an SJE context requires that your students feel safe enough to be their full selves, and that they are not punished for being who they are.

From radical love, we move clockwise to cultural competence, for if love is the highest level of understanding between individuals, then their various cultural identities must have space to breathe, grow, and thrive in the classroom. In practice, that means understanding your own culture(s) and biases, while being familiar with various aspects of students' cultural differences, and how those cultures might be expressed. From cultural competence, we continue clockwise to CRT. CRT is a legal theory developed in the late 1970s that specifically focuses on the permanence of racism through the law and *interest convergence*. The concept of racism being permanent is directly connected to the material aspects of white supremacy. As such, the term interest convergence, coined by one of the CRT founders, Derek Bell, posits that Black people only achieve civil rights when it serves the (material) interests of white people.

Although CRT was primarily discussed in legal scholarship, prominent education scholars like Gloria Ladson-Billings began to draw connections between CRT and education, specifically, as many of the ideas presented, were relevant in many classrooms: the permanence of racism, unfair policies, and practices that harmed our most vulnerable (Black, Indigenous, and people of color, BIPOC) students and putting the interests of testing companies over the well-being of a holistic approach to students' ever-changing needs in a culturally, racially and linguistically diverse society. In scholar Gloria Ladson-Billings' ground-breaking article, "Just What is Critical Race Theory and What's It Doing in a Nice Field Like Education?" (2010), it is noted that, "Critical race theory sees the school curriculum as a culturally specific artifact designed to maintain a white supremacist master script" (p. 19). In other words, the curriculum is the gateway to maintaining and upholding white supremacy and an anti-social justice approach to teaching and learning, as a result.

Current debates about CRT have come to dominate national headlines due to the way it has been framed by state legislatures in relation to classrooms and teaching subject matter like racism, slavery, and social justice (Schwartz, 2023). These debates illustrate the CRT tenet of interest convergence, as many policymakers see no value in teaching about the history and permanence of racism in schools since it does not provide any material or financial benefits to said states. CRT emphasizes that race and its byproduct, racism, are socially constructed and deeply ingrained in our nation's institutions including the way we *do* school.

Last, but certainly not least, we move clockwise to student visibility, which denotes a student-centered approach to teaching and learning that honors student voices and their respective forms of cultural capital. Each of these puzzle pieces fit tightly yet imperfectly together, comprising and sustaining an SJE framework. Always keep in mind that living a life intentionally grounded in social justice will come with its own ongoing battles due to the ways that racism and classism sustain the current balance of power in our country. As such, fighting for equity also threatens capitalism, the root of the American economy. Some of you may be thinking, is this worth the fight? And this is what I want you to know, if your freedom becomes more relevant than my freedom, then the condition of our overall and collective humanity will continue to deteriorate. An SJE approach to teaching and learning has the power to elevate education while transforming our respective communities, families, and institutions. Therefore, creating a social justice-inspired classroom ultimately creates a more humanizing and psychologically safe society. As writer and activist James Baldwin said, "We can disagree and still love each other unless your disagreement is rooted in my oppression and denial of my humanity and right to exist." Centering student voices and lived experiences honors their basic humanity while creating space to build relational trust over time through love.

All of this is encompassed by radical love. When we radically love our students, we can really *see* them for who they are, authentically and holistically. The lenses of CRT, cultural competence, and student visibility ground my social justice approach to pedagogy by elevating love, kindness, respect, and honesty, all of which start outside of the classroom; it starts in the mirror. Some teachers will say, "But if I honor who they are and they do something *wrong*, how is that okay?"

This is an example of a fixed mindset, and it is the antithesis of love. Simply asking students to stop "bad behavior" doesn't work. Instead, as educators, we must model intentional and radical acts of love that show up for students even when they do not show up for themselves. Quite often, students do not yet have the tools necessary for radical healing, whether it's from low self-esteem, disengagement, or feeling overwhelmed. The reality is that most human beings have endured some form of trauma throughout their lives—some more than others, of course. Social isolation among Black students is well-documented even among the most elite high schools in the country (Samuel & Wellemeyer, 2020), and racial stress at school is reported by Black children as young as four (Anderson & Stevenson, 2019). Recent systematic reviews of literature on childhood trauma have also shown that educators who try to remain "race-neutral" or "race-evasive" often amplify childhood trauma about racism and its connection with school and even federal policies (Alvarez, 2002). Therefore, we must provide our students with the social, emotional, and metacognitive tools necessary for encouraging their own healing. Our best response to a student "doing something wrong" is to show radical love in this way.

PORTRAITURE AGAINST OPPRESSION

With the pillars of our SJE framework from Chapter 1 in mind, I now want to introduce the research component of my SJE framework through narrative inquiry, a critical component of *portraiture*, a research method developed by Harvard sociologist Sara Lawrence-Lightfoot.

Portraiture is a creative "method of inquiry and documentation in the social sciences that combines systemic, empirical description with aesthetic expression, blending art and science, humanistic sensibilities and scientific rigor" (Lawrence-Lightfoot & Davis, 1997, p. 3). Unlike more traditional research methods, portraiture centers narrative inquiry and human observation as a primary lens for seeing and making sense of the world. The creator of portraiture is Sara Lawrence-Lightfoot, an American sociologist at Harvard University who studies the connections among schools, education, and social change. As such, her most popular books explored the interactions among teachers, students, families, and communities, as a way to examine how to improve teaching and learning environments.

Portraiture speaks to an SJE framework as it seeks to disrupt, humanize, and reimagine what schools can become if only we listen with intent and observe with love and intentionality. Similar to portraiture, an SJE framework honors students' cultural ways of knowing and being as the groundwork for creating deeper relationships inside and outside of the class-room for lasting change and critical transformation.

As you continue your journey into this book, narrative, research, and *science* (I mean this in the *softest* of ways, i.e.: the valuing and understanding of the power of human emotions and stories, a form of *emotional science*) will intersect to help you uncover your role in your respective organization with regard to SJE.

You may be wondering if you are in fact a social justice educator. Or, you may be nodding your head in agreement thinking, "Of course, I am a social justice educator." As I write this book, we are living in one of the most oppressive political landscapes in American history. Children are dying at the hands of Immigration Customs & Enforcement (ICE) at the border (Acevedo, 2019) and the uteri of immigrant mothers' are being forcibly removed without consent (Lithwick, 2020). Simultaneously, Supreme Court Justice Ruth Bader Ginsberg, the second woman to serve on the United States Supreme Court and a deep advocate of social justice and equity-based policy initiatives passed away, changing the overall dynamic of the Supreme Court, undermining much of the progress that had already been made during her tenure. At the same time, Black men like Jacob Blake (another unarmed Black man) continue to be murdered by police. Blake was shot seven times in the back by police in Kenosha, Wisconsin in 2021, as his three Black sons were seated in the back seat of his SUV. The time to stand up for justice is always now.

To be a social justice educator is to not only be armed with this information but to know how to use it as a current affairs curriculum in your classroom on a day-to-day basis. We cannot claim to be social justice educators without addressing, in our classrooms, the day-to-day racial and cultural warfare students encounter. So, I pose this question to you: Are you ready to not only discuss oppression but actively work against it in your classroom through how you teach and what students learn? If your answer is yes, then you are ready to endure the hard work of sustaining a social justice educator community within your respective school, organization, or institution. We are collectively responsible for eradicating political, racial, economic, and educational oppression through social justice teaching and learning practices.

FREEDOM, LIBERATION, AND RADICAL LOVE ENGAGEMENT

Let us return to our hearts for a second. Implementing and thriving within an SJE framework is heart work. Works of the heart expose our vulnerabilities while awakening what we know to be true: that we all deserve to teach, learn, and grow within educational spaces that allow us to be *free*. As we know, acts of freedom look different depending on who you are: your racial/ethnic background, your class, your sexual orientation, and your gender identity, to name a few critical identity markers. If we do not feel free within ourselves or within the spaces where we work, how can we possibly provide a sense of freedom for our students?

I discussed the heart chakra and its association with compassion, love, and empathy in the Introduction. When our heart chakras are fully opened, we experience a sense of awakening. Zen priest Angel Kyodo Williams discusses the significance of being "awake" and its connection to having a "warrior-spirit" in her book, *Being Black: Zen and the Art of Living with Grace and Fearlessness* (2002). Williams notes, "warriors live a life of action and clear direction. We can bring warrior-spirit to the cause of peace and harmonious connection because it is about life and living, not power and aggression" (2002, p. 66). For us to provide spaces of freedom for our students to be their authentic selves, we must first awaken our "warrior-spirit" by looking in the mirror and asking ourselves these questions which I call "The RLE Check-In."

1. Do I feel free in my body on a daily basis? How does this impact how I interact with and my ability to love my students?

2. Am I making space for students to challenge my ways of knowing in the classroom?

3. What are some of my fears in the classroom and how are my fears a reflection of my biases?

Embodied teaching through radical love is the process of acknowledging the ways our feelings, emotions, intuition, and physical bodies impact how and what we teach. Embodied teaching is directly connected to what I call Radical Love Engagement, which is a concept that explores authentically embracing our intersectional identities in the classroom as a way to get students to embrace their full selves, too. The moment we enter the classroom, we are bringing an intersectional self that includes the physical, emotional, and spiritual aspects of our respective identities. When we can embody our full selves in the classroom, our level of RLE with students, as well as their engagement levels, will increase. RLE is similar to embodied teaching in the sense that we acknowledge the physical body and our emotional selves as an aspect of the teaching and learning process. What makes RLE different is a direct focus on loving all of ourselves through embracing our various identities. When we love ourselves fully (including our flaws) we are able to love students for their authentic selves, as well, not only when they do things to please us or adhere to the status quo.

In scholar and cultural critic bell hooks' seminal text *Teaching to Transgress: Education as the Practice of Freedom* (1994), she describes a similar embodied teaching approach which she refers to as engaged pedagogy. The main premise of engaged pedagogy is the process of centering students' voices in the classroom and curriculum while encouraging a mutual exchange of vulnerability. Similarly, RLE requires that we are vulnerable, as deep love encourages the ability to become and be softer with ourselves and others. When we can be vulnerable in a way that honors our authentic selves, we can experience what is called liberatory pedagogy, which is the application of teaching and learning to embrace freedom.

When we can be vulnerable in a way that honors our authentic selves, we can experience what is called liberatory pedagogy, which is the application of teaching and learning to embrace freedom.

To further expand on education and liberatory pedagogy, I turn to hooks (1994) engaged pedagogy:

When education is the practice of freedom, students are not the only ones who are asked to share, to confess. Engaged pedagogy does not seek simply to empower students. Any classroom that employs a holistic model of learning will also be a place where teachers grow and are empowered by the process. That empowerment cannot happen if we refuse to be vulnerable while encouraging students to take risks. . . .I do not expect students to take any risks that I would not take, to share in any way that I would not share. (p. 21)

Therefore, to practice the art of SJE is to dance with freedom. Such a dance encourages us to practice letting go of our assumptions while exploring our inner and outer biases. It asks us to step into a mutual exchange of multiple forms of knowledge with our students. Intimate dances with freedom are really at the heart of teaching and learning for social justice. Think about how much we can do when we are not fearful, but free. When we are not merely tolerated, but accepted. Removing fear and accepting our students and ourselves for who we are is the foundation for love and logic in the classroom, especially radical love.

WHAT ARE YOU WILLING TO LOSE?

What is SJE? Up to this point, we have seen that it encompasses the practice of radical love, intersectional and cultural understanding, CRT, student visibility, and the willingness to fight oppression in the classroom by openly discussing race, ethnicity, culture, and other elements of personal identity. It requires that we dance with freedom and be vulnerable with our students so that they can be vulnerable with us, which means it involves enabling our students to be themselves in our classrooms. An SJE requires taking risks, standing up for what is right, and quite often, it also requires being unpopular in order to create more spaces of liberation for our students in schools. To create more equitable schooling systems, we must be willing to lose some of our privileges that reify the status quo, such as using a non-diverse curriculum and stifling students' voices to maintain power and control.

But this alone is not enough. To become a social justice educator, one must be able to look in the mirror and examine their inner-self. If you cannot look closely at who you are, how can you possibly model radical self-acceptance for your students? Now, to be clear, becoming a social justice educator does not require you to be a perfectly whole human being, for all of us are broken in some way: by time, tragedy, suffering, love, and loss. In *Hope and Healing in Urban Education* (2016), Shawn Ginwright draws on the idea that many social justice educators become invested in this work due to their own pain and personal traumas. As he speaks with a local community organizer, the role of healing in activist work is highlighted:

> You know 80% of the movement is us fighting among ourselves because a lot of people bring all their cargo - all their baggage into the circles. So there are a lot of wounded people in the social justice movement. That's why they are passionate about justice because they have been wounded. They are trying to stand up for justice but they still haven't healed up and they are bringing it and they are projecting it and there are a lot of internal divisions. (p. 134)

Similarly, we all carry our own personal, political, and practical baggage. We must be willing to understand these aspects of ourselves, for they are the gateway to understanding others, especially our students. As many of you may have experienced during your journey into teaching, our students will enter the classroom with their baggage, and you will enter with yours. The key to bridging these generational, cultural, economic, and racial divides includes pausing and asking ourselves: What am I willing to lose to bridge these gaps? Portraiture is an entry point to creating intentional opportunities for critical observation, creativity, and honoring our collective humanity to impact social changes that will create a more equitable world. Using portraiture as a research method creates space for critical and radical storytelling that illustrates the complexities of teaching and learning in a social justice context.

What am I willing to lose to bridge these gaps?

To begin, we must be willing to lose our biases; we must be willing to lose our pride; and, most importantly, we must be willing to lose our sense of control over every situation. Our desire to control our classroom environment, especially as teachers, often stimulates oppressive teaching and learning practices. When we let go of the need to control our students, they become more trusting in our classrooms due to the outward and intimate display of love for them on a daily basis.

An SJE employs an intimate display of love for students that includes:

1. Daily affirmations
2. Emotional and academic support
3. Regular communication with parents, guardians, and caretakers
4. Sharing resources for activities outside of school and in the surrounding community
5. Connecting students with the right people/organizations in order to help develop their knowledge-base and talents

These five key acts of love and life are the foundation for becoming and sustaining your ongoing journey as a social justice educator. However, doing them well requires that you let go of things you might have thought were important for a successful classroom. Loving your students is essentially the ability to put them before yourself when making curricular and social-emotional learning decisions. Are you ready for that kind of radical commitment in your life? When we make a commitment to being and becoming a social justice educator, it requires daily intentionality in our lived experiences both personally and professionally.

RADICAL LOVE REFLECTION: KEY ACTS OF LOVE

When people used to ask me what I taught, I would often say that apart from being an English teacher, my main goal was teaching students about loving themselves more. This happened after years of witnessing brilliant, talented Black and Brown students think of themselves as inferior due to the emotional and structural violence that shaped many of their schooling lives. Their emotional health came first because I understood that without addressing their emotional health, their academic health would continue to suffer. I came up with a game plan that began with daily affirmations. Every morning, there were inspirational quotes on my whiteboard meant to inspire self-love in the hearts of my students. These quotes were always in the same place, on the left-hand side of the board with the words "Affirmations" at the top. These daily affirmations would cultivate conversation among my students inside and outside of my classroom. Sometimes it was connected to my lesson, however, many times it was not. Rather, these affirmations made them reflect on their personal lives and how they saw themselves in school and in their respective communities.

I offered a lot of emotional support and gave students opportunities to change their seats or take breaks when they needed one. I want to be honest and share that these practices were not popular at the time; however, they centered my students' humanity while making them feel safe in my classroom. They would share stories with me about their personal lives and ask me for advice. If I could offer some immediate advice, I often did. If I believed they could benefit from speaking with the school counselor, I would bring the counselors in, as well. In fact, I had to strengthen my relationship with the school counselors in order to fully and holistically support my students.

Thanks to many of my mentors, I created open door policies for parents to text or call me (during school hours and up to 5 p.m.) to learn more about what their students were learning or if they had concerns about their students' social activities, as well. I would often call parents with good news, so that when bad news did come up (because that is part of the job, too) it did not feel like an attack, but rather an ongoing conversation on how to best support the needs of the students. I also updated online grading often so that parents could see how their children were progressing on a daily basis and they were encouraged to reach out to me if they were worried about particular grades and student behaviors that were documented on the online grading platform.

I shared opportunities for students to explore their own communities, which was easier for me since I always lived close to the communities, I taught in. In fact, I ran into many of my students doing simple things like grocery shopping or taking the subway. I used my own knowledge of the surrounding community to encourage students to become more interested in the local opportunities surrounding them every day. For example, I had a group of students use video cameras to capture an aspect of their community that they loved. This seemingly simple project created opportunities for personal storytelling and filmmaking, making students feel loved and respected. For many of them, it was the first time they were asked, "what do you love about your neighborhood?"

Similarly, I would also partner with other organizations like the Tribeca Film Festival and the Hip Hop Theater Festival to create unique internship opportunities for students to explore new interests outside of their communities to strengthen their creative and intellectual lenses.

My deep love of my students was personal because I remembered being a young Black girl in Brooklyn, New York, finding my way and wanting to excel academically and socially. My education offered me many pathways for success and my main goal for becoming a teacher was to offer that to more students who looked like me in historically underserved communities.

EQUITY AND EQUALITY: REPRODUCING THE STATUS QUO

Another key aspect of adopting an SJE framework is to understand that equality and equity are not the same. As our society continues to advance in the areas of technology and a more inclusive approach to education, the terms equity and equality are often conflated in educational research and discourse. The distinction between the two terms is critically important whether you are an educator, school leader, or an educational researcher.

Put briefly, equality aims to ensure that everyone operates from the same level or on an equal playing field. To strive for equality is to strive for equal treatment of all. Equity, on the other hand, involves recognizing that we do not all start from the same level and that we cannot, because of various social realities, all play on equal ground. Depending on the families we were born into or raised by, there are socioeconomic inequities that we cannot avoid. Equity aims to rectify that by giving individuals what they need to succeed based on where they are within that socioeconomic reality.

I will begin with an anecdote to help you distinguish the two. Starting in kindergarten and going up through the eighth grade, I was tracked as a gifted student. This meant that I was in all honors classes with teachers who were specifically selected to teach students like me, who performed well on standardized exams and assimilated easily into the cultural norms and acceptable behaviors of public schooling in New York City. As a child, I knew that I was in the "top" class, because we often heard the teachers talk about this, sometimes to our faces and sometimes in jest to colleagues during our lunch period. In many ways, the dialogue around who we were as students was connected to merit and honor.

As a result, we were afforded more privileged schooling opportunities. We went on more field trips than other students, we had access to foreign languages and computers, and we learned in cohorts, which meant that we followed each other year to year, keeping the group as exclusive as possible. Rarely did a new student join our cohort and rarely did one of us leave. These precious "gifted" spots were held for *special* students who could easily model the language and norms of the NYC public schools, norms that largely mirrored white, middle-class expectations about education, employment, and career-making.

Rather than an example of equitable education, I have come to understand that this exclusive gifted education model was oppressive because, "to oppress is to hold down-to press-and deny a social group full access and potential in a given society" (Sensoy & DiAngelo, 2017, p. 61). The gifted students in my school were provided with ample opportunities to learn outside of school, to experience an academically rigorous curriculum, and to challenge one another's thinking in the classroom, thus building their cultural capital. Students outside of these courses had significantly fewer opportunities to engage in schooling of the same caliber. The opportunities I had were provided directly by the school but only to a limited few. This learning hierarchy had both short-term and long-term consequences for everyone in the school, whether they were a part of the gifted education program or not. Those who were not a part of the program were still directly impacted due to limited resource allocations.

Educational disparities like this are rampant in the United States, particularly in communities that serve Black, Latinx, and Indigenous students, and they exist within rural communities as well as urban ones. Recent educational data reveals that "systemic patterns of racial socioeconomic inequality drive inequalities across multiple educational outcomes" (Shores et al., 2019, p. 1). In other words, BIPOC are automatically at a disadvantage the moment they enter schooling systems because schools mirror systemically inequitable practices like redlining (Coates, 2015), limited access to affordable healthcare, and high levels of police brutality (Peeples, 2020). Schools then become a site where the status quo is reproduced. More specifically, systemically oppressive pedagogy becomes the norm in schools through grading disparities (Feldman, 2018), hidden curricula (Anyon, 1980), and learning practices that are neither culturally responsive nor oriented toward social justice.

Fast forward to 30 years after I graduated from my gifted program. A large percentage of the students who were tracked with me in those courses went on to successful careers in education, finance, and hospitality, to name a few. At the same time, a large percentage of students who were not in our gifted courses went on to struggle both financially and personally. Some lost their lives, some were incarcerated. A few from that group managed to find their footing in various corporate sectors, as well as in civil servant work, becoming postal workers, police officers, sanitation workers, train and bus operators, etc. I did not have this language at the time, but it is clear as day to me now that the magnet school I attended growing up in the Ditmas Park/Flatbush section of Brooklyn, NY was, as social reproduction theory calls it, reproducing the status quo.

Students (like me) would presumably succeed due to our ability to assimilate to school norms through the likes of standardized testing and behavioral compliance. This is one of the ways that social inequalities are reproduced from one generation to the next (MacLeod, 2008). Students like me were modeling middle-class ways of knowing and being through "concerted cultivation" (Lareau, 2003), which is a parenting style that fosters the development of children's perceived talents through organized activities. The gifted education teachers at my school used this parenting style in a school setting by creating more opportunities for organized activities outside of school, but it was solely for the gifted students. From a social justice standpoint, one can say that the teachers were modeling acts of love through teaching and cultivating extracurricular and co-curricular activities, but only for some.

These activities were exclusive to gifted students with high standardized test scores, thus replicating a social hierarchy within the school similar to the one exhibited by the 1% of Americans who hold the majority of the country's wealth (Ingraham, 2017). Thus, we cannot discuss equality in education without addressing equity. Where and how we begin as people and as students is really the luck of the draw. We can begin to level the playing field created by socioeconomic circumstances by creating spaces in schools that foster equity for all students, not just those lucky enough to be born into the right circumstances. This can then lead to conditions of equality through social justice leadership practices that inspire radical and transformative teaching and learning experiences from the inside out.

UNLEARNING THROUGH HEALING

In the article "Whose Culture Has Capital? A Critical Race Theory Discussion of Community Cultural Wealth," CRT scholar Tara Yosso (2005) shifts the narrative that marginalized communities, particularly in urban school districts, are inherently disadvantaged. Rather, those who reside and are schooled in marginalized communities are expected to adhere to the norms of the middle and upper class as a way of fitting into school systems that privilege labor over love. Yosso offers an alternative perspective called Community Cultural Wealth, which includes different forms of capital that elevate the diverse experiences that BIPOC students bring to the classroom. An example of Community Cultural Wealth includes aspirational capital, which is the ability to maintain hope for the future, even in the face of deep adversity. Aspirational capital is important for many BIPOC students, since "CRT suggests that current instructional strategies presume that African American students are deficient" (Ladson-Billings, 2016, p. 25). If teachers operate from spaces where they view their students as "empty vessels to be filled with knowledge" (Freire, 1968), then classrooms become sites of oppression rather than sites of love.

During my tenure as an English teacher in NYC public schools, the concept of deficit thinking was the norm for many educators, especially when applied to students who were BIPOC. I continued to witness this deficit thinking as I expanded my work with large school districts nationwide. Such thinking is typically grounded in the assumption that the only people responsible for a child's education are their parents and the students themselves, regardless of where they live and learn. Although many of the students and their families I have worked with had aspirational and familial capital, in cases where students did not produce high scores on standardized tests, some administrators and teachers believed it proved their intellectual inferiority (almost always in comparison to white students). As such,

> for the critical race theorist, intelligence testing has been a movement to legitimize African American student deficiency under the guise of scientific rationalism (Alienikoff, 1991; Gould, 1981). According to Marable (1983), one purpose of the African American in the racial/capitalist state is to serve as a symbolic index for poor Whites. If the working-class white is 'achieving at a higher level than Blacks, then they feel superior. This allows Whites with real power to exploit both poor Whites and Blacks. (Ladson-Billings, 2016, p. 26)

The construction of whiteness as the standard for excellence in our society is directly reflected in our schools, and it harms all of us of every race, class, gender, and socioeconomic status (SES), as it reproduces white supremacy. To counteract this, we must be mindful of the immediate methods by which we reproduce injustice and hierarchy through inherently oppressive schooling structures. We can, for instance, see the oppression in instructional practices that privilege Westernized ways of knowing and being through the study of (mostly) European history, culturally *unresponsive* ways of knowing, and the desire to control students' physical bodies and minds. To adopt an SJE framework that intentionally disrupts oppression and centers student voices (especially those that are typically at the margins of presumed competence, such as BIPOC), requires unlearning through healing practices that model radical love through social justice, a culturally relevant curriculum and student-centered approaches to learning.

The following activity is an example of creating spaces for students to engage in SJE practices through critical thinking and observation. The intentional use of images connected to current events helps provide cultural and social contexts for the state of our society. It provides students an opportunity to see themselves as critical change agents who have a voice and an obligation to leave the world better than they found it.

This activity is also an example of portraiture, as it sets the context, revealing that "the portraitist is not only interested in recording the contemporary physical setting, she also wants to sketch the institutional culture and history-the origins and evolution of the organization and the values that shape its structure and purpose" (Lawrence-Lightfoot & Davis, 1997, p. 52). Such a research-based activity will allow teachers to gain important knowledge regarding their students' perspectives and lived experiences, which will deepen relational trust, creating more psychological safety in the classroom and the overall school community at large.

RADICAL LOVE ACTIVITY #2: THE EQUITY V. EQUALITY BAROMETER

Grades 5–12 (Please scaffold activities according to grade level. For lower elementary grades, options 4 & 6 are the best options).

Learning Objective: Students and teachers will analyze a series of images and identify whether they believe each one represents an equity or equality issue.

Radical Love Goal (RLG): To have a critical understanding of SJE, students, teachers, and administrators must know the distinctions between equity and equality.

Students will be presented with various images related to equity or equality that have recently had a major impact upon our schools and communities nationwide. The pictures will be taken directly from current events that are directly connected to the educational and political landscape such as:

1. The Capitol Insurrection of 2021
2. The impact of the Coronavirus on public school reopening plans nationwide
3. The murders of Breonna Taylor & George Floyd
4. Food swamps & food deserts in rural & urban communities
5. Local images of the school and how it has changed (or not) over time
6. Local housing & healthcare options for families
7. The long-term impact of the Coronavirus on learning outcomes for all students
8. Student sexualities and identities in the school curriculum
9. Special Education in public schools
10. The school-to-prison pipeline

Students will choose an image/number that resonates with them, and teachers will divide them into groups based on their respective choices. In student groups, they will be responsible for discussing the following questions:

- Is this topic directly connected to equity and/or equality? How do you know?

- Why did you choose this particular topic?

(Continued)

(Continued)

- Have you had an opportunity to discuss this topic in school before? If so, explain. If not, why do you think that is the case?

- Please share any additional thoughts or insight you may have pertaining to this topic.

Total Activity Time = 30 minutes

Whole Group Share: Each group will have five minutes to share what they discussed in their respective group using ideas from the graphic organizer they used to answer the questions (see end of the chapter for sample graphic organizer). While the groups are sharing, students are encouraged to listen and take notes on any new information they did not know beforehand, based on what is shared.

Activity Debrief, Questions and Summary

Students will have an opportunity to discuss their perception of the activity in relation to equity and social justice frameworks. Students will discuss some of the glows and grows that occurred as they worked with others in topic-based groups. Glows are things that really went well and grows are things we can get better at doing.

1. What did you learn as you completed this group assignment?
2. How did you work with your classmates in a collaborative fashion?
3. Did you all have similar views about equity versus equality? Explain.
4. If you could, would you change anything about this learning activity?

Extension Assignments

Grades 5–12 (Please scaffold activities according to grade level)

1. Using the photos you viewed in class today, choose three of these photos to write a position paper discussing the connections between equity and social justice in the classroom. Think of a personal learning experience in your life to support your position.

2. Choose a Science, Technology, Engineering and Mathematics (STEM) content area. How do any of these photos connect to math and science education? Think of a personal learning experience that can speak to your connections between the images and the STEM-related content area.

3. Come up with a community project where you choose one of the photos and interview two to three people in your community about their understanding of what they see. The purpose is to explore

common threads as well as diverse perspectives on social justice issues (Figure 2.2).

FIGURE 2.2 • Note-Taking Graphic Organizer

QUESTION	REACTION	SOCIAL JUSTICE CONNECTION
Is this topic directly connected to equity and/or equality? How do you know?		
Why did you choose this particular topic?		
Have you had an opportunity to discuss this topic in school before? If so, explain. If not, why do you think that is the case?		
Please share any additional thoughts or insight you may have pertaining to this topic.		

Throughout this chapter, you have journeyed with me through the layers of SJE and the intentionality needed to make it come to life. As we channeled the waters of CRT, we were confronted with the harsh realities of racism that impede success for Black and Brown students in many classrooms across the nation. As such, to teach is to acknowledge the ways that intersectionality plays a role in how we show up in the world and why it is important to see our students as multifaceted people who have much to offer in the classroom. None of us are one thing, we are many things, complex, beautiful, and ever-changing.

When we actively enact an SJE framework in our classrooms, we are developing spaces for liberation while molding the change agents we have the opportunity to teach every day: our students. While we are teaching them, they are also teaching us about confronting our biases, pushing against the status quo, and using RLE to be more honest, more vulnerable, and less afraid to stand up for what is right. As we begin to truly see our students as more than a test score or a skin color or a socioeconomic background, our students will also truly see us as more than enforcers of rules, but as leaders who have their best interests at heart.

Analyzing images is a powerful way for students to heighten their senses of how they see and understand the world based on who they are, where they live, and the opportunities that are provided through schooling on a daily basis. With the current prevalence of book banning nationwide (Pendakahr, 2023), there is a limiting mindset that discussing social justice is harmful to young people or that it can be "too early" to discuss. That is in fact untrue and underestimates the power students have to transform the world by providing pedagogical opportunities to become more critical of their environments while thinking of ways to disrupt the status quo, a critical aspect of SJE.

CHAPTER 3

Heart Healing Through Teaching, Leading, and Unlearning

Love and justice are not two. Without inner change, there can be no outer change. Without collective change, no change matters. (Angel Kyodo Williams)

RADICAL LOVE NOTE #3

Broken hearts can heal if we are willing to nurture them. Too many broken hearts are living and learning in school buildings.

These hearts are tested every year.

These hearts are often stifled by assessments that do not **see** them.

These hearts sometimes prepare lessons with trepidation instead of freedom as school leaders are encouraged to do **more**, **more**, **more**, at the expense of their backs and their collective breath.

And when the test results are released, some school buildings are closed or turned around by the states, so these hearts are faced with the impact of policies that bleed out onto the concrete surrounding the schools. The trauma surrounding the drama of learning, from job precarity to racial discrimination and inherently inequitable policies, becomes the cataclysmic soundtrack to many students' and teachers' lives. In the middle of all this, we must remember one critical piece of this educational puzzle: healing.

Our educational healing must be centered on the learning, as we are all wounded composites of the time we have been given thus far. How we teach is directly connected to the depth of our radical healing, and therefore how students learn depends on our ability to heal and to transform that healing into pedagogy centered in equity. For us to teach and learn in a way that humanizes everyone, healing social justice practices are not only necessary but critical for leaders, teachers, and students, especially because our educational systems are filled with historical patterns of oppression. Working within systems of oppression and remaining committed to social justice methods rooted in radical self-care and community requires an almost Herculean effort. Such work is often the reason we need healing so desperately. Most of us learn how to survive oppressive practices without dismantling them, but a social justice mindset requires dismantling oppression at the root in order to achieve true and lasting liberation.

What must we dismantle to win our freedom? How can we heal from our own internal traumas to be the best educators for our students? How can we teach students to heal themselves through teaching, learning, and radical love? Come with me into this critical consciousness landscape to find out.

Chapter Objective

In this chapter, there is an intentional focus on the significance of unlearning when it comes to social justice education because we cannot learn new things if we are unwilling to let go of what we think we already know. Through the concept of unlearning, there is a shift to our hearts as the gateway to implementing more liberatory teaching and learning frameworks into our classrooms and ways of knowing. As such, I touch on meritocracy and why it is directly connected to upholding inequity and the status quo while providing new social-justice-aligned strategies such as a socio-cultural consciousness approach that focuses on how our differences and lived experiences shape how we teach and how we learn. Through a sociocultural consciousness approach, I share student anecdotes as a way to lean into their stories (through my lenses—which is connected to a portraiture research framework that honors context and obser-vations) that have shaped my own perceptions and understanding of teaching and learning, based on my experiences as an educator in various spaces for over 16 years.

Finally, I explore Critical Race Theory (CRT) which essentially names the permanence of racism due to the history of oppression and systemic inequality that perpetuates white supremacy in the ways we *do* schooling in this country. Having a deeper understanding of CRT, especially in this current political climate where it is deemed a threat as opposed to a learning tool, can allow educators to identify the ways that systemic oppression has become the norm inside and outside of the classroom. I offer a tool I developed called an Equity Action Plan (EAP), which allows leaders to implement a plan to undo harmful teaching and learning practices that disrupt the status quo. I wrap up with a Professional Learning Community activity to encourage leaders to directly implement a strategic action plan.

UNLEARNING INEQUITABLE PARADIGMS

As we continue to lean into the social justice education framework as broken down in Chapter 2, let us go back to the center of our hearts. The heart and the brain are the parts of ourselves that allow us to *unlearn*. The unlearning process is crucial to adopting a social justice education framework since we must be willing to release the oppressive ways of knowing and being that we have been indoctrinated by, often through the schooling process itself. To unlearn, we must shift our mindset.

Mark Bonshek, Chief Epiphany Officer of Shift Thinking, described unlearning in an article in the *Harvard Business Review* as "the ability to choose an alternative mental model or para-digm. When we learn, we add new skills or knowledge to what we already know. When we unlearn, we step outside the mental model in order to choose a different one" (2016). In that article, Bonshek describes how he learned to drive a car while visiting Great Britain. Getting used to driving on the left side of the road, he says, was easy. But unlearning all the ways in which driving on the right side of the road impacted his brain was hard. In more sophisticated cases, like long-held views about educational assessment and grading, community involvement, or racial prejudice, unlearning is even harder. Unlearning isn't subtracting knowledge, but it does involve learning how old systems of thought fail to serve teachers and students.

In school cultures nationwide, learning is a process of adding new knowledge, often as a way of confirming dominant biases and ideologies. Ideology is typically described as the beliefs and principles held by an organization or group of people, especially a political party. But in *Is Everyone Really Equal: An Introduction to Key Concepts in Social Justice Education* (Sensoy & DiAngelo, 2017), ideology is analyzed from a social justice perspective and described as "a powerful way to support the dominant group's position." In many ways, this mirrors sociological understandings of ideology, which define it as the "cultural beliefs that justify particular social arrangements, including patterns of inequality" (Macionis, 2010). In concert with this definition, Sensoy and DiAngelo continue: "There are several key interrelated ideologies that rationalize the concentration of dominant group members at the top of society and their right to rule" (p. 17). Such ideologies are reinforced by everything from mass media to religious institutions, business relationships, and education. To push against dominant group ideologies centered in white supremacist ways of knowing and being, which are repeated within school culture and school curricula, we must consistently be in a state of unlearning. This unlearning process will shape our ability to expand our critical consciousness through our vulnerabilities and our unique lived experiences by removing the so-called facts and accepted wisdom passed down through the mechanisms of inequitable ideologies (like mass media and education) and allowing us to see the subject with fresh eyes. It will also require aligning our push for social justice education with antiracist teaching and learning models that emphasize equity through inclusive classroom practices.

MERITOCRACY AND DOING SCHOOL

One such inequitable ideology is *meritocracy*, and it is essential that we understand it in relation to unlearning and social justice education. Sensoy and DiAngelo define meritocracy as, "the belief that people's achievements are based solely on their own efforts, abilities or merits" (p. 91). The notion of meritocracy is a direct threat to implementing social justice teaching and learning practices as it functions under normative conceptions of schooling that reinforce a "one-size-fits-all" approach to education. Rather than acknowledging the forces that inequitable learning environments exert on different students, schools, and communities, this ideology sees success as the product of individual and isolated effort. When teachers fail to consider the cultural backgrounds of their students, or they fail to recognize the funds of knowledge those students bring to the classroom through their social and familial experiences, they emphasize the expectation and belief that students begin from an equitable playing field and have access to all the resources that make success within this system possible. But we know this is not the case. As reported in EdWeek:

> A 2016 synthesis of decades of research on culturally responsive teaching and related frameworks found that engaging in culturally affirming practices across subject matters, including mathematics and science, led to positive increases in students' understanding and engagement with academic skills and concepts... Culturally responsive teaching and similar approaches to teaching also increased students' motivation, interest in content, and the perception of themselves as capable students, among other benefits. (Will & Navarro, 2022)

In other words, students succeed through their own efforts but require the skills and abilities of teachers, family, and community members who can respond to their needs and interests.

Meritocratic practices affect our schools in other ways too. In her book *Doing School: How We Are Creating a Generation of Stressed-Out, Materialistic, and Miseducated Students* (2003), veteran teacher and author Denise Pope follows five successful students in high school for an entire year. She learns through their stories how they were socialized into *doing school* rather than learning. In this sense, *doing school* connotes all the actions students perform to *succeed*, as opposed to actions they would perform to learn, grow, change, and become freer individuals. In essence, these students had learned that manipulating the educational system to get high grades offered immediate and palpable rewards. Worse still, they often sacrificed their own physical and emotional health, as well as their own ethics (e.g., cheating on homework and tests), to get ahead in the name of achievement and educational "success." Many schools reward similar behavior, promoting a culture of meritocracy that ignores the many personal dimensions of student and human life. This is another example of ideology that is eerily reminiscent of the 1% capitalist model: success above all else, even the well-being of others.

SOCIOCULTURAL CONSCIOUSNESS

This culture of *doing school* reinforces extreme codes of conduct such as zero-tolerance policies that incorporate punitive and exclusionary discipline practices, especially in urban school districts, while adhering to standardized testing and teacher-centered pedagogical practices (often rote and disengaging) that typify meritocratic ideologies. Instead of modeling teaching and learning practices that embrace meritocracy and "pull yourself up by your bootstraps" conservatism, educators can embrace a social-justice-oriented approach through **sociocultural consciousness**, an aspect of a culturally responsive paradigm. Sociocultural consciousness is the "awareness that one's worldview is not universal but is profoundly shaped by one's life experiences, as mediated by a variety of factors, chief among them race/ethnicity, social class, and gender" (Banks, 1996; Bennett, 1995; Cochran-Smith & Lytle, 1993; Sleeter, 1992). When we understand that our lived experiences are inherently shaped by our respective identities (race, class, gender, ability, and sexuality), we can cultivate a more humane approach to the students, fellow educators, and community members who may be different from us. In essence, developing sociocultural consciousness allows us to break out of the meritocratic mode by centralizing the roles that others play in our development as students, educators, and individuals within the community. What does this look like in the classroom? Let us begin to dissect what it means for teachers to embrace sociocultural consciousness.

SOCIOCULTURAL CONSCIOUSNESS IN THE CLASSROOM

I will always remember Kendrick, a student I met during my first year of teaching. An 8th grader small in stature, yet big in ideas, especially when it came to art, Kendrick was always drawing. During my lessons, he was creating images of some of his favorite comic book characters. In his reading journal, which we used daily, I would find drawings everywhere, surrounding his words.

As a first-year teacher working under oppressive conditions, where teaching to the test was the norm, Kendrick's insistence on drawing when he should be "learning," bothered me, and disrupted the flow that I created to have my students follow a routine that made sense to me but not to many of them. My teaching routine was focused on grades and scores, even though my heart knew this did not feel good. Why did I do this? Because administrators were in my classroom daily, hovering over me, ensuring that I was aligned with the pacing calendar and raising student scores. This constant pressure made students like Kendrick seem like a threat to me, even though he had much to teach me.

One day, I asked Kendrick why he was always drawing instead of doing the assignments. Kendrick answered, "I don't know...I like drawing." A simple response. A response that touched me because I knew Kendrick liked school and wanted to be there. He just needed a way to become more engaged and my heavily meritocratic lessons surely were not helping. Because I was also in graduate school at the time, earning a Masters in the Science of Teaching, I was learning more about sociocultural consciousness and culturally relevant teaching and learning practices. As a result, I decided to allow Kendrick to add drawings to his writing assignments, to merge what he loved with what we were learning. His drawings had to illustrate his words so that I could assess whether or not he understood the reading comprehension strategies I was teaching. It was a slow process, however, over the course of a month, we developed a routine that made more sense for Kendrick. He would begin each day by writing his response to the quote on the board, a critical analysis technique I used daily to encourage students to write more. The quotes were usually provocative and pushed them to reflect upon their lives. One of the quotes I used was James Baldwin's famous words, "To act is to be committed, to be committed is to be in perpetual danger." I asked students to first explain the quote and then express how it was directly connected to their lives. Kendrick described the highs and lows of living in a low-income community and feeling misunderstood in school and at home. He then drew a superhero-style figure, who represented himself and his super strengths. For Kendrick, commitment meant expressing himself through drawing and reimagining what his life could become if given an opportunity. He did not see himself as the petite 14-year-old who appeared before my eyes, rather, as a strong hero in charge of naming his identities.

We can develop our sociocultural consciousness in the classroom by listening to our students and creating curricular opportunities that elevate their creative and cultural gifts. Kendrick was the first student I fully listened to while shifting my curriculum to speak to his needs because I valued him as a student and as a person in the classroom. When we value our students for who they are, we can create a curriculum that allows opportunities for freedom and growth, key aspects of embracing social justice education through sociocultural consciousness.

SEGREGATION STILL SHAPES OUR BELIEFS

We can first begin with a deeper understanding of nationwide demographic schooling data to get a sense of who is in the classroom with regard to race and ethnicity. Acknowledging who is in our classrooms provides a macro context for the environments in which educators and students develop their sense of self.

According to the National Center for Education Statistics (NCES, 2021), "in fall 2018, of the 50.7 million students enrolled in public elementary and secondary schools, 23.8 million were White, 13.8 million were Hispanic, 7.7 million were Black, 2.7 million were Asian, 2.1 million were of two or more races, 0.5 million were American Indian/Alaska Native, and 186,000 were Pacific Islander."

The following chart, also from the NCES (NCES, 2023), shows how often students in those groups attend schools with other students from the same (or similar) racial/ethnic background. For example, only 22% of Black students attended schools where 75% or more of the school population were of the same race/ethnicity. But 44% of white students attended schools where 75% or more of the population were of the same race/ethnicity, and a further 33% of whites attended schools where white students comprised at least half of the student population. In contrast, 60% of Black students attended schools where they comprised less than half of the student population and 61% of Asian students attended schools where they comprised less than 25% of the students at that school (Figure 3.1).

These data also reveal that white students make up the largest single racial group in the schooling population and that "compared to White students, a higher proportion of students of color attended schools in which the combined enrollment of students of color was at least 75 percent of total enrollment in fall 2021" (NCES, 2023). Only 23% of white students attended schools where less than 50% of the school population was white, and only 6% attended schools where white students represented 25% or less of the school population. This segregation of Black, Indigenous, and people of color (BIPOC) students and white students has been an ongoing trend since at least the 1980s, something researchers at The Civil Rights Project connect with residential segregation across the country. In fact, it has been noted that schools are more segregated today than they were in the 1960s. According to a 2019 article in the *New York Times* titled "Still Separate, Still Unequal: Teaching About School Segregation and Educational Inequality," "'More than half of the nation's schoolchildren are in racially concentrated districts, where over 75 percent of students are either

FIGURE 3.1 ● Percentage Distribution of Public Elementary and Secondary School Students, by Student's Race/Ethnicity and Percentage of Student's Own Racial/Ethnic Group Enrolled in the School: Fall 2021

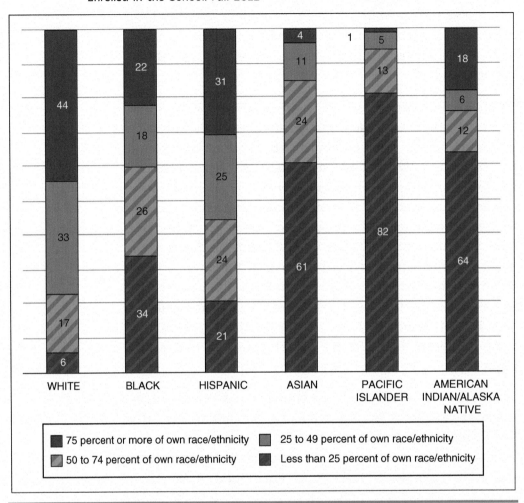

Source: U.S. Department of Education, National Center for Education Statistics, Common Core of Data (CCD), "Public Elementary/Secondary School Universe Survey," 2021–2022. See Digest of Education Statistics 2022, Table 216.55. Also available at https://nces.ed.gov/programs/coe/indicator/cge/racial-ethnic-enrollment

white or nonwhite'. In addition, school districts are often segregated by income. The nexus of racial and economic segregation has intensified educational gaps between rich and poor students and between white students and students of color" (Meatto, 2019).

The essential social justice questions I want you to consider here are these: How do segregated school districts impact our ability to develop a healthy sociocultural consciousness? How does this impact our social justice teaching and learning models?

How do segregated school districts impact our ability to develop a healthy sociocultural consciousness? How does this impact our social justice teaching and learning models?

If the majority of students nationwide only have opportunities to interact with others who more or less have the same racial/ethnic and socioeconomic background, we must assume that their knowledge of those who are different from them is coming from less reliable, often biased sources: from television, from social media consumption, from generational ideologies passed down within families, and from the surrounding communities, the last of which is also known as racial socialization. Scholar Enrique W. Neblet, Jr. explains that "racial socialization refers to the process by which race-related messages about the meaning of race and racism are transmitted by parents intergenerationally" (Neblett et al., 2016). As such, parents have their own social justice responsibilities that include discussions around inclusivity and racial/cultural differences that come up daily in the classroom. To illustrate this point more clearly, teachers need to develop equitable relationships with parents to help counter false intergenerational beliefs about race that are elevated by propaganda. Some examples of this include inviting parents into the classroom often (not only for parent–teacher conferences), as a way to build transparency about teaching and learning practices, while valuing their insights and perspectives. Another example of including parents more directly in the education process is having "positive phone calls," a practice where I would call parents to share something wise their child said or did in the classroom, specifically around an assignment that was social justice inspired. A social justice-inspired assignment is one that incorporates differentiated learning practices, student autonomy, and socially relevant themes connected to race, class, gender, and ability. As a result, I was able to cultivate deeper relationships with parents that allowed us to agree and disagree on key social justice issues while focusing on the overall well-being of their child and our school/classroom communities. Schools must operate as sites of continuous learning not only for students and staff but for parents, as well, to build inclusive communities that honor parents as critical stakeholders in the educational process.

EXPANDING OUR CONSCIOUSNESS

It is also important to identify how the perspectives of racially dominant groups come to limit (and therefore define) the perspectives of other groups, especially when it comes to education and the understanding of our own histories. This requires a CRT lens, since CRT focuses on how the permanence of racism in American culture and society perpetuates white supremacy. Predominantly white schools represent an unspoken standard for curriculum in this country and are therefore treated as more valuable by educators because they uphold the white supremacist values at the root of most curricula nationwide. Education scholar Gloria Ladson-Billings explains that "CRT sees the official school curriculum as a culturally specific artifact designed to maintain a white supremacist master script" (1998, p. 18). Dominant groups achieve this primarily by means of omission, which is what Ladson-Billings has in mind when she uses the term "master script." It has a special meaning in this case: the silencing and erasure of perspectives of non-dominant races and cultures from the curriculum. This is achieved in a variety of ways. For example, stories of African Americans go missing from the curriculum or are otherwise altered to suit the beliefs and feelings of the dominant culture. Thus, Ladson-Billing continues, "Rosa Parks is reduced to a tired seamstress instead of a long-time participant in social justice endeavors... Or, Martin Luther King, Jr. becomes a sanitized folk hero who enjoyed the full support of 'good Americans' rather than a disdained scholar and activist whose vision extended to social justice causes throughout the world and challenged the USA on issues of economic injustice and aggression in Southeast Asia" (p. 18).

Remember that the majority of teachers in the United States are white (79% in 2018), and it is no secret that school curriculum nationwide privileges Eurocentric ways of knowing and being that essentially erases or homogenizes the experiences of BIPOC students. It does this in a variety of ways, from treating academic English as a default language for all academic pursuits to abiding by laws that forbid teaching American racism and slavery in classrooms, as the wave of anti-CRT legislation demonstrates. Several states have actually banned CRT from being taught in schools, along with banning books that discuss racism in American history. For example, in the state of Tennessee, "the law limits how teachers can discuss racism" (Anti-Defamation League, 2021). As such, a group of parents in Tennessee wanted to ban a book about Ruby Bridges, the first Black child to attend and desegregate an all-white elementary school in Louisiana. Similarly, in Houston, Texas, a group of parents created a petition to cancel an in-person appearance by award-winning author Jerry Craft, because they believed his graphic novels promote CRT. One of Craft's books, *New Kid*, explores the lived experiences of a 12-year-old African-American boy who experiences culture shock when he attends a predominantly white private school. Anti-CRT legislation and parent groups that mobilize to remove books about racism from the curriculum, shut down critical conversation, and cut the development of a sociocultural consciousness in half before it can even begin to grow.

In opposition, applying both CRT and a social justice lens to our schools and curricula expands our sociocultural consciousness. It emphasizes knowledge as a social construction rooted in power and privilege and encourages us to interrogate it. Why do we teach this way? Why do we forbid some subjects and promote others? These are questions we can answer. But how does social justice education achieve this and thereby create a more inclusive environment? How does it shift our perspectives and foster a sociocultural consciousness rooted in genuine interactions and encounters?

To answer that question, we begin by acknowledging that resources are more abundant in predominantly white school districts, almost always as a result of higher property taxes, stronger healthcare systems, and better access to quality food. In other words, we must understand that structural inequities impact our sociocultural consciousness too. Predominantly Black schools and schools with majority BIPOC student populations are often part of communities that lack fair housing, have inequitable access to healthcare, and subsist within food deserts. These are inherited qualities that result from our country's history of institutionalized racial discrimination, including slavery, redlining, and the white flight that followed the Great Migration out of southern states. The perception of these schools and communities is often guided by opinions about the individual members within them and the choices they make. But we must break that tendency and understand instead how systemic racism, white supremacy, and mastering scripting have engendered these conditions, whatever the behavior of the individuals born into it.

"CRT argues that inequality in school funding is a function of institutional and structural racism... Without suffering a single act of personal racism, most African Americans suffer the consequence of systemic and structural racism" (Ladson-Billings, 1998, p. 20). For example, in *Connecticut Coalition for Justice in Education Funding (CCJEF) vs. Rell*, it was revealed that higher-income cities and towns spent as much as $6,000 more per pupil each year than higher-poverty areas. Such discrepancies, it was revealed, occurred because most public school districts in America are run and funded by local resources. As Alana Semuels reported, "High-poverty areas such as Bridgeport and New Britain [in Connecticut] have lower home values and collect fewer taxes, and so can't raise as much money as a place like Darien or Greenwich, where homes are worth millions of dollars" (2016). In 1973, the Supreme Court heard *San Antonio Independent School District v. Rodriguez*, in which a father sued the state of Texas with such inequities in mind, pointing out that schools were funded in a way that violated the US Constitution's equal-protection clause in the 14th Amendment. The Supreme Court disagreed even though, in 1972, Richard Nixon had commissioned a report that found inequitable distribution of funding to schools "according to the needs of children." Rather than funding education at the local or municipal level, it recommended the collection and distribution of funds to districts by the states. This recommendation was ignored, and the Supreme Court ultimately left the issue of education funding up to the states. States, however, are hesitant to redistribute funds from rich neighborhoods to poor ones. As Semuels points out, "It may seem logical that a state would step in and try to fund poorer districts; states don't want to be known for low test scores and graduation rates and will pay the price if their residents don't get a good education. But giving money from rich districts to poor ones is politically difficult... And money is increasingly tight as states struggle with budget issues and have to spend more money on corrections, infrastructure, and Medicaid than they once did" (2016). In 2018, the Connecticut Supreme Court ruled in favor of the state, arguing that no equal rights protections had been violated, thus leaving the issue of more equitable funding up to the legislature and prolonging a systemic issue with roots in redlining, industrialization, and regional inequalities that grew in the wake of World War II (Semuels, 2016).

But the disparities among Black and white school districts illuminate a much deeper history behind the Black and white wealth gap, which is the direct effect of inequality and discrimination dating back through 246 years of chattel slavery. According to McIntosh et al. (2020) of the Hamilton Project, an economic policy initiative, "This history matters for contemporary inequality in part because its legacy is passed down generation-to-generation through unequal monetary inheritances which make up a great deal of current wealth." Framing the history of economic inequality is important for understanding the inequities present in classrooms nationwide as it directly impacts education. To ignore the history upon which the United States was founded, and to ignore the consequences of that history, is to sit in a space of complacency that places dominant culture (re: constructions of whiteness and white supremacy) at the helm. Sociocultural consciousness leads us out of that complacency.

This, of course, calls into question racist tropes that educators encounter every day. For instance, knowing how structural inequities impact the lives of BIPOC students and their families, we can ask probing questions about the so-called "learning" or "achievement gap" between white students and BIPOC students (basically anyone who is not white). Is it fair to compare students in wealthier school districts to students who have a history of economic disadvantages? What is the stated purpose of such a comparison? And does it matter given that it only centers on white supremacy? After all, whatever changes a district might make in response to these gaps, BIPOC students must also face those changes as "proof" of deficit conceptions about their abilities and backgrounds, particularly if they go to school in economically disadvantaged districts.

RADICAL LOVE REFLECTION: GAPS V. INEQUITIES

My initial training as a teacher in New York City through Teach for America positioned students as "levels" as opposed to people. Students were identified by test scores and other standardized testing data as a way to determine how they should be taught or how they should learn. This felt unnatural to me and downright inhumane. I was determined to learn more about students, families, and communities for who they actually were, as opposed to what I was being trained and prepared to believe. The most important goal appeared to be raising their test scores to measure growth and academic achievement. However, there was a lack of attention placed upon their social-emotional growth, genuinely caring for them, and loving them. Everything I was witnessing as a first-year teacher embodied students as numbers to be raised. My heart chakra became closed off and I knew I had to do something different if I wanted stronger holistic outcomes for my students that were not solely connected to their academics but also to their emotional and social well-being.

Instead of falling into the harmful mindset of a so-called "achievement gap," I began to reimagine these gaps as inequities due to limited resources, the top-down curriculum that was teacher-centered, and school cultures that overemphasized controlling students' bodies through detention and strict classroom rules to remain seated at all times.

I started by reimagining the scripted curriculum I was mandated to teach by shifting the lessons to meet the learning objective while making the lessons more engaging through a student-centered approach and adding more culturally responsive texts that spoke to students' daily realities. For example, I would incorporate "Warm Up" writing that always required students to focus on something in their own lives and then make connections to the texts we were reading. I also used hip-hop music (which many loved) to draw on various concepts in English literature such as figurative language and plot development. Students became more engaged day-by-day until they were eventually rushing to come to my class. When students felt valued and were taught that their voices mattered, they became more academically engaged and more connected to school overall. We must take time to stop viewing students as a gap to fill and rather disrupt systemic inequities to provide more engaging teaching and learning practices.

I use the terms Black/white and BIPOC interchangeably in this book because such terminology is rooted in CRT and in my lived experiences. I use them to describe the ways that chattel slavery has disproportionately impacted the experiences of Black folx for centuries and because the historical reality of how the United States came to be (via the institution of slavery) is reflected in conceptions of Black (or BIPOC) vs. white. Prolific CRT scholar and one of its original founders Derrick Bell notes in his masterpiece, *Faces at the Bottom of the Well: The Permanence of Racism* (1992) that "we must see this country's history of slavery not as an insuperable racial barrier to Blacks, but as a legacy of enlightenment from our enslaved forbears reminding us that if they survived the ultimate form of racism, we and those whites who stand with us can at least view racial oppression in its many contemporary forms without underestimating its critical importance and likely permanent status in this country" (p. 12).

The permanence of racism in the United States is a central tenet of CRT, as it draws on historical contexts that speak to the fact that racism is a lucrative game that benefits the oppressor (dominant culture/re: white culture) while keeping the oppressed (BIPOC, with an emphasis on anti-Blackness) at the margins.

Therefore, it is important for me to use the terms Black, white, and BIPOC as a way to honor my lived experiences and radical truth, while at the same time acknowledging a more inclusive and present-day framework rooted in social justice practices.

At the same time, I understand, as a Black woman, that everything is not Black and white, literally and figuratively.

Making space for other voices of color at the margins (Latinx, Native American, Asian, and multiracial) does not require that we eliminate the Black and White narrative. Rather, the broader narrative is connected with and exists alongside the familiar narrative of Black and White. Using an intersectional lens rooted in CRT and intersectionality requires that we name and share the complexity of what it means to belong to a group outside of the dominant one, and it is important that we understand how *othered* groups use labels in their own writing. Expanding our consciousness requires sensitivity and openness to everyone impacted by many effects of racial discrimination and white supremacy.

DISRUPTING THE STATUS QUO

School segregation is a social justice issue. While changing ourselves and expanding our sociocultural consciousness is important, we cannot change schools without changing the communities that surround them too. We cannot change education without making quality school access a civil right for everyone involved. It is hard to believe that the Brown V. Board of Education case of 1954, which aimed to desegregate schools 70 years ago, has still not yielded desegregated schools and school districts in the United States. At this moment, let us pause to ask ourselves, if the judiciary system ruled in favor of desegregating schools, why was/is it that in practice this policy did not yield the expected results?

Many musings and theories come to mind but the reality is this: white people were not ready for desegregation, as is clear from the way many southern communities resisted integration. And when white people are not ready for a change (the end of slavery, reconstruction, school desegregation, etc.), the opportunity for change and all it can bring evaporates. In this chapter, we have mentioned some of the many ways white people hold positional power across important equity access industries, whether it's in relation to equitable housing, healthcare, access to food, or education (even in cases where those white people claim to be acting in the interest of everyone) and systemic issues such as these perpetuate further inequities. How can we begin to address this network of inequity?

As the concept of sociocultural consciousness suggests on its own, and as the first pillar of my framework instructs, we can start by learning more about one another and our various access points to privilege based on our respective backgrounds. A social justice education provides us with the foundational learning blocks to help us thrive individually and collectively, within and across race, class, gender, sexuality, and ability.

But reading about these issues in the abstract is sometimes misleading and can keep us from understanding and internalizing the lessons we need to learn and internalize. We can often gain clearer insight into these national (and universal) problems by looking at how they've affected us personally. Using CRT and portraiture, I want to present a vision of education that harmonizes how we learn with how we feel. I want to us to use the social justice education framework to put our hearts and personal experiences at the center of our response to white supremacy so that we can heal, unlearn, disrupt, and ultimately surmount the difficulties posed by segregation, meritocracy, wealth inequity, and other forms of systemic racism. To illustrate this process and how it leads to revelations about our educational system, I will relate to you some of the experiences with racism and school inequity that I remember from my own education. I will then show how these revelations connect to recent educational policies, which have, under the guise of supporting student achievement, continued to reproduce a status quo that is damaging to all students, but especially BIPOC students.

MANIFESTATIONS OF THE STATUS QUO IN TEACHING AND TESTING

I learned the differences in school quality and access first-hand growing up in the Flatbush section of Brooklyn, which at the time was truly a mixed-income community. There were Hasidic Jews on one side, Caribbean and West-Indian immigrants on another side, and white people in between who could afford the large pre-war homes on the tree-lined streets of Dorchester Road and Ocean Avenue. That area, now commonly referred to as Ditmas Park (affectionately referred to as Flatbush when I was growing up, and still is by the Black folx who reside there), is named after Jan Jansen Van Ditmarsen Jr., an early Danish settler who had a colonial style farmhouse on the corner of Flatbush Avenue near Ditmas Avenue and who owned a large portion of property in Ditmas Park. It is hard to believe there was ever a farmhouse anywhere near Flatbush Avenue because, when I was a child, it was lined with Caribbean restaurants, dollar vans that would take people up and down Flatbush Avenue from Kings Plaza to Downtown Brooklyn, and a large cluster of Caribbean and African immigrant homes. My family was one of these Caribbean transplants, who immigrated to the United States in the early 1970s from the small Island of Trinidad & Tobago, a twin-island Caribbean nation near Venezuela.

As a first-generation Caribbean American, my early experiences with schooling (and for most of my academic career) were rooted in notions of meritocracy: just work hard and everything will come to fruition. As we discussed earlier, meritocracy reinforces the idea that one can achieve anything one desires solely through hard work. College admissions scandals in recent years have shown that wealthy white families stand to benefit most from this ideology because they can literally pay to appear worthy of merit. Research in the last two decades has continued to show how the concept of meritocracy greatly benefits white people, especially cisgender white men because they belong to the dominant racial group and have the most interest in maintaining the status quo (Knowles & Lowery, 2012). This was just as true when I was younger. As a result, I was socially conditioned to enter the school system (that was not designed for me or people like me) with the notion that, if I worked hard enough, I could eventually make enough money and, one day, have property to call my own. I believed in the meritocracy myth because it is what my teachers and family presented to me, and my immigrant family believed in education as the equalizer for our success in the United States because the country promotes itself in exactly that way. It is a similar narrative delivered to and believed by immigrant families all over the world.

To be fair, my education has taken me to new spaces and places and in some (but not all) cases improved my overall quality of life. I constantly remember the words of my teachers, also echoed by teachers today: "If you work hard, you will do well in life." The focus on hard work as a direct extension of schooling and being successful in life seemed fair enough. I never questioned if it was equitable because I did not yet have those lenses growing up as a Black girl in Brooklyn, New York in the 80s–90s.

I understood school as something to *do*, something to be *good* at while making yourself and your family proud. You did not critique the school or question school leadership because there was an automatic *trust* in schooling systems as the backbone of individual success in my family. But the beginning of my social justice education and sociocultural consciousness started in school. I began to question everything when I realized I was treated differently by many teachers and school staff because I was an outspoken and smart Black girl.

When I began to share stories with my mom about how teachers would accuse me of "talking too much" (despite the fact that I had straight A's) or being "sassy" or simply calling me out in front of the class for no reason, her response was almost always "take it easy and focus." I know my mother meant this in the most positive way, based on her own lived experiences and cultural ways of knowing and being. However, I did not know what to do with this advice because the *act* of schooling often seemed robotic to me, with occasional highlights with fun activities like: Picture Day, Field Day, or the most fun of them all: when your least favorite teacher is absent and you have a substitute for the day. But, of course, I listened to my mother and kept up the politics of respectability that was attached to school. The politics of respectability as I remember them were as follows:

1. Listen to the teacher (no matter what they say)
2. Never question a teacher because that is a sign of disrespect
3. *Trust* the teacher because they have your best interests at heart

The politics of respectability in my direct consciousness almost always centered on the teacher. The teacher was the first point of reference, the person you went to when you needed help, and the person who held the most immediate *power*. This was also connected to my cultural ways of knowing because, for my mom, everything always came back to, "Well, what did the teacher say?" or "Did you listen to your teacher?" Narratives that solely focus on teacher actions continue to be a norm among students and families, as if teachers operate alone as opposed to within educational systems that replicate the status quo and model the hierarchy established within our capitalist society. Teachers are directly connected to the overall school culture, which includes leadership practices and opportunities for growth through professional learning.

But placing the blame on teachers for every problem in schools is like blaming 99% of the world's population for issues that 1% of the population has control over. Policymakers and state officials often pass oppressive policies that directly impact teaching and learning, so teachers do not always have a direct impact on what is expected of students (or of themselves), yet they are often blamed for low outcomes connected to academic achievement and overall student success. To further expound upon this point, the Obama Administration launched the $4.35 billion Race to the Top (RTT) initiative in 2012, which aimed to increase student academic outcomes by focusing on "*teacher effectiveness*, using data effectively *in the classroom*, and adopting new strategies to support struggling schools" (White House Archives, 2012, emphasis mine). There were also performance incentives for teachers who showed the most growth based on standardized test scores in particular areas (English Language Arts and Math). Applications for funding were based on several different criteria but forced states to compete with one another based on benchmarks like "Improving teacher and principal effectiveness based on performance" and "Supporting the transition to enhanced standards and high-quality assessments." Essentially, President Obama's initiative reproduced the educational status quo by aligning money with student academic outcomes. The table below illustrates how states were evaluated by specific criteria in Phase 1 and Phase 2 of the initiative (Figure 3.2).

FIGURE 3.2 ● Race to the Top Point Allocation for Applications With Selection Criteria and Descriptions

SELECTION CRITERIA	DESCRIPTION	TOTAL POINTS POSSIBLE
State Success Factors	Articulating the State's education reform agenda and Local Education Agency's (LEA) participation in it; Building strong statewide capacity to implement, scale up, and sustain proposed plans; Demonstrating significant progress in raising achievement and closing gaps (30 points)	125 points
Standards and Assessments	Developing and adopting common standards; Developing and implementing common, high-quality assessments; Supporting the transition to enhanced standards and high-quality assessments	70 points
Data Systems to Support Instruction	Fully implementing a statewide longitudinal data system; Accessing and using State data; Using data to improve instruction	47 points
Great Teachers and Leaders	Providing high-quality pathways for aspiring teachers and principals; Improving teacher and principal effectiveness based on performance; Ensuring equitable distribution of effective teachers and principals; Improving the effectiveness of teacher and principal preparation programs;	138 points

(Continued)

Figure 3.2 *(Continued)*

SELECTION CRITERIA	DESCRIPTION	TOTAL POINTS POSSIBLE
	Providing effective support to teachers and principals	
Turning Around the Lowest-Achieving Schools	Intervening in the lowest-achieving schools and LEAs; Turning around the lowest-achieving schools	50 points
General Selection Criteria	Making education funding a priority; Ensuring successful conditions for high-performing charters and other innovative schools; Demonstrating other significant reform conditions	55 points
Priority 2: Competitive Preference Priority	Emphasis on Science, Technology, Engineering, and Mathematics (STEM)	15 points, all or nothing

Source: U.S. Department of Education (2009).

Each category measures student success based on common core state standards, effective leadership, rigorous academics (particularly in STEM), and supporting "low-achieving" schools." However, conditions for creating equity and culturally responsive education are missing entirely.

Education reform policies often focus on a supposed lack of academic achievement in our most underserved schools instead of carefully evaluating the root causes connected to inequality in the surrounding school community, another echo of the meritocratic structures that control our schools. As such, policies like former President Obama's RTT reinforce the status quo by blaming the schools themselves for poor test scores, instead of recognizing the systems that create cycles of dysfunction and low student achievement.

To make matters worse, the primary form of assessment emphasized by the initiative was state standardized exams, which are known to be culturally biased and a poor reflection of student intelligence and academic readiness. As Kyung Hee Kim and Darya Zabelina explain in *Cultural Bias in Assessment: Can Creativity Assessment Help?*:

> Standardized tests intend to measure intelligence and general knowledge, but they are normed based on the knowledge and values of the majority groups, which can create bias against minority groups, including gender, race, community status, and persons with different language backgrounds, socioeconomic status, and culture. (Kim et al., 2015, p. 129)

Standardized tests do not account for multiple learning styles, a diverse set of lived experiences, or for students who speak multiple languages. Of course, we need standards to hold our educational system accountable for high expectations for all students nationwide, but the rigidity of the standards does not abide by a social justice framework and fails to account for the many different ways students show up to school: culturally, emotionally, physically, and spiritually. Part of the necessary work entailed in modeling social justice ways of knowing and being in schools requires acknowledging students' full and authentic selves, which are not solely rooted in academic achievement. The Social Emotional Learning (SEL) aspects of an individual are just as important as the academic characteristics that make up student learning and achievement. As Meg Anderson related in a recent National Public Radio (NPR) article, all 50 states have standards related to SEL in preschool, and more than half of US states have standards at the K-12 level. Numerous studies have found that SEL programs are effective and contribute to higher academic achievement, higher graduation rates, and even the acquisition of stabler jobs later in life. Despite this, conservative activists and representatives have attempted to curtail social-emotional learning in concert with their attacks on CRT, often conflating the two. Reasons vary from state to state, but we can see an element of white supremacy here in their insistence that identity, social justice, and multicultural education don't belong in classrooms. It's the perpetuation of the meritocratic ideology we have discussed and a reinforcement of the white, cis-gendered, largely male status quo that affects so much of educational policy. No wonder, then, that leaders within the Florida Department of Education were worried that some social studies textbooks might result in "student indoctrination:" fear of indoctrination against the status quo is all but stated explicitly (Anderson, 2022).

MANIFESTATIONS OF THE STATUS QUO IN SCHOOL LEADERSHIP

School leadership is equally as important as teachers when it comes to fighting for equity and the success of all students. I can honestly say that, as a Black girl growing up, the phrase "go to the principal's office" was riddled with fear (and still is). Therefore, never being in the principal's office was considered a *good* thing because it meant that you were "doing well and following protocol." Fear of school leaders is the norm in many school districts, which eliminates the opportunity for a humanizing kind of leadership, where there is freedom to critique existing systems for the sake of more equitable teaching and learning environments for everyone: students, parents, teachers, and leaders.

Providing school and district leaders with professional learning opportunities that focus on a leadership equity model can foster a reimagination of what leadership can look like, shifting the emphasis from spaces of authority to spaces of love. An equity leadership model "provides leaders a framework for creating a learning environment where students, across their many differences, engage deeply and achieve at higher levels while staying true to who they are" (Gogins, 2021). Once leaders are prepared to see the value that students already bring to schools, they can create equitable conditions to ensure student success that embraces their diverse lived experiences. But first, school/ district leaders must reflect on their own biases and how it impacts the decisions they make and the interactions they have with others. The next step is acknowledging how racism impacts the school culture and climate. Once leaders have the space to self-reflect and make a direct connection to how racism shows up in their schools, districts, and communities, they can then take a deeper look at school/district-wide policies and practices to determine if they are equitable and meet every student's needs. A commitment to equity requires deep self-reflection and immediate iterative changes reflected in the overall school culture through policies, pedagogy, and practices.

In my previous role as a Director of Partnerships for a non-profit education organization, I worked with medium-to-large school districts to implement literacy curricula through equity frameworks. To position equity in a more intentional way, I developed an Equity Action Plan (EAP) to support school and district leaders as they implemented literacy through equity frameworks. One of my continuous struggles while leading this work was helping leaders and coaches follow through with equity practices on the ground. Seeing this work through is much easier said than done, especially since it requires us to be self-reflective and acknowledge our own biases.

How can we effectively merge culturally responsive leadership theories with equitable practices that are measurable and sustainable?

My EAP helps leaders do just that. By using it, leaders can brainstorm, evaluate, and prepare an action plan that merges theory and practice for equitable and sustainable student outcomes. The goal of the EAP is to scale for equity for all students on a continuous cycle of improvement (on a quarterly basis). The EAP note catcher illustrated below explains step-by-step how leaders should approach the plan as a tool for effective leadership transformation (Figure 3.3).

Please use this Equity Note Catcher to document how you plan to implement equity frameworks in your school district/school.

Equity Action Plan

E = *Evaluate* how your teachers/school currently navigate and co-create the school climate for equity outcomes

A = *Assess* district glows and grows to determine potential leadership-based action steps to create equitable school cultures

P = *Prepare* a leadership plan that elevates district/school needs through a commitment to creating an equitable school culture that intentionally disrupts systems of oppression

FIGURE 3.3 ● Equity Action Plan Overview

3-POINT PLAN BRAINSTORM	REFLECTIONS AND ACTION STEPS
E = *Evaluating* where your teachers currently are in navigating and co-creating the school climate for equitable outcomes	**E = *Evaluating***
A = *Assessing* district glows and grows to determine potential leadership-based action steps to create equitable school cultures	**A = *Assessing***
P = Preparing a leadership plan that elevates district/school needs through a commitment to creating an equitable school culture that intentionally disrupts systems of oppression	**P = *Preparing***

 Available for download at **resources.corwin.com/RadicalLove**

WHAT CAN I DO NOW?

So where do we go from here? Now that I have shared some of the complexities of 21st-century school segregation, the presence of institutional racism in our schools and communities, and educational policies that ignore the root causes of some of our most persistent problems, ask yourself: where do you see yourself in this equation? Sometimes, it is easier to view the issues as an outsider, but we have to admit and know how we relate to these issues as educators, teachers, leaders, researchers, and parents/guardians. This is what will ultimately help us transform our educational landscape as a collective. I want you to go back to the concept of *unlearning* presented at the beginning of the chapter and reflect on it. Then, I want you to ask yourself the following questions:

1. What do I need to unlearn to support a social justice education framework in my school community?
2. How can I recognize the cultural value and funds of knowledge (Moll et al., 1990) students bring into the classroom space as a curricular tool?
3. What are the culturally responsive and equitable conditions for success in my classroom?

Asking yourself these questions will begin the process of heart healing through teaching and learning. This process requires your radical honesty to build the sociocultural consciousness needed to not only practice social justice education ways of being in schools but also become a model of social justice. This is no easy task because you will experience heartbreak due to the various ways systemic racism divides us-a harmful experience for all of us. The good news is that healing is often on the other side of heartbreak and we need to heal our hearts in order to teach and learn with love, social justice, and equitable student-centered practices.

RADICAL LOVE ACTIVITY #3: HEART CHAKRA HISTORIES

Learning Objective: Principals and school administrators (Deans, Instructional Leaders, and Coaches) will examine their personal histories and trace the trajectories of their pathway to leadership.

Radical Love Goal: School leaders are critical to the overall success of implementing a social justice education framework. Giving leaders the space to examine their hearts will lead to their social emotional growth and development, a key example of social justice leadership practices.

School leaders will be placed in pairs to discuss the lived experiences that led them to leadership careers. These discussions will set the stage for an identity-mapping activity grounded in cultural competence. Cultural competence is the ability to build authentic

(Continued)

(Continued)

relationships across cultures, which effective leaders must possess to lead with love and equity.

Total Activity Time: *60 minutes*

Leadership Pair Questions: *10 minutes*

Leaders will respond to these questions in pairs. Time should be set aside for professional learning to complete this workshop activity.

1. Where did you grow up as a child?

2. How do you self-identify when it comes to race, class and gender? Did you imagine you would become a school leader? Explain.

3. What makes your leadership style unique?

4. What strategies do you use as a leader to ensure equitable success for all students, especially when faced with challenging circumstances?

Activity Debrief and Summary Questions: *20 minutes*

1. How did your heart feel while doing this activity with a colleague? Why?

2. What would you like to become stronger at as a leader when it comes to creating equitable leadership practices?

3. How do you think your own personal histories impact your leadership style?

Extension Leadership Activity: *20 minutes*

Overview: Becoming a culturally competent leader requires having a clear understanding of one's own identity in relation to others. Fostering more authentic relationships across cultures can create and sustain more inclusive and socially just learning communities in schools.

Activity: Identity Chart

Each leader will create an identity chart with their respective names in the center. Leaders will then fill in with words they use to describe themselves as well as words they believe other people use to describe them. Leaders should come up with at least 10 words for this activity. Five of the words should be words they use to describe themselves. The remaining five words should be words that others often use to describe them. Please see Figure 3.4 for a sample identity chart I created as a model of how to complete this activity.

FIGURE 3.4 ● Identity Map

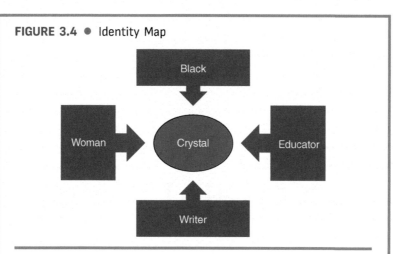

 Available for download at **resources.corwin.com/RadicalLove**

Post Assignment Share-Out: 10 Minutes

Leaders will make space to share their identity maps with one another to build a Radical Love Leadership Community (RLLC). A RLLC honors the hearts and well-being of all participants and acknowledges that a radical love requires collective healing, unlearning, and sociocultural consciousness to elevate the overall school community to which participants belong and co-create as leaders. Learning more about one another's respective identities will lead to stronger leadership practices that are grounded in collaboration and humanity. Leadership identity charts should be stored in a safe space where leaders can review them on a continuous basis to be mindful of their own identities in relation to others. The goal is that this kind of RLLC will be modeled to teachers, who can then model leading with love, equity, and intersectional identities to students (Figure 3.4).

Throughout this chapter, we have explored the intersections among unlearning, sociocultural consciousness, and pushing against inequity through our collective humanity. In order to change the status quo, particularly in education, we must develop a clear understanding of how CRT plays a role in how we see ourselves in relation to others. Developing a more critical and conscious understanding of ourselves and others will help to cultivate stronger education leaders and as a result, more culturally responsive teachers, leading to effective social justice education-oriented classrooms for the overall benefit of our students.

CHAPTER 4

Special Education and Social Justice

It is not possible to be a teacher without loving one's students. (Paulo Freire)

RADICAL LOVE NOTE #4

Like many teachers, I was unprepared to teach students with special needs until I was faced with my own students with special needs. It was the year 2008, just two years after I entered the teaching profession. After teaching in a "high-needs" school, I was now in a new school in New York, recently founded by a young principal with a big vision: integrate arts into the curriculum to boost student achievement. The student population was not much different from the previous school, mostly Black or Brown and from the surrounding community: Bedford-Stuyvesant, Brooklyn, aka Bed-Stuy. Most of the students were eligible for free and reduced lunch and all of them were seeking a quality education to transform their lives. They may not have said it directly, but their actions always spoke for them. The saying, actions speak louder than words, is one that I had to learn more intimately as a teacher. I had to develop an understanding of what the students needed even though the students may not have been able to articulate it themselves. And this uncovering of their deepest needs through the intuitive realms of my teacher's heart is what kept me teaching, even on days when it seemed impossible.

Since I was certified as a secondary English teacher in the state of New York (7–12) and was typically placed with "General Education" students (a name I dislike; there is nothing general about any of us), I had never been faced with intentional planning for students with special needs. I did not have a Special Education background, nor did my experiences as a Teach for America Corps Member (06') prepare me for supporting them. So how did I learn? Like many teachers do: on the job. That first year at Brooklyn Love School (BLS) was different in a good way. Everyone appeared to be committed to helping students become their best selves. We often worked collaboratively and had a continuous cycle of professional development. But nothing quite prepared me for teaching a quirky ninth grader who I will call Othello. Dark-skinned, wide-eyed, and socially awkward, Othello appeared to be a 14-year-old teenager with Asperger's Syndrome. His social awkwardness caused tension in the classroom, as students reflect the society they live in, there was a constant clash between Othello's interests and the interests of students who are used to functioning within an ableist framework. Othello's extreme fascination with trains took over almost all lessons, leading students to roll their eyes whenever he spoke. The more I tried to create a more inclusive environment for Othello and other students like him, the more I drowned in overworking to create more engaging and culturally responsive lessons. It was all too much sometimes: the grading, the behavior management, the oppressive school system and structures, the test preparation that made everything feel bland. . . I could not protect Othello from bullying and from feeling ostracized for most of his high-school career. I could not protect Othello from the community he lived in, which seemingly betrayed him for being obviously different. And this is why I start with this anecdote. Because I want to remember how I became better by messing up. I want to remember how humbling it was to work with Othello every day and unlearn some of my own biases about students with special needs. He was brilliant and eager to create, discuss, and think deeply about all things, trains and films. However, the social struggles he faced made his academic successes seem insignificant to him. Othello wanted more friends, he wanted to be accepted in popular social circles. And in his own way, he was.

He eventually became popular for being openly different, which of course has pros and cons. On one hand, you can inspire others to be themselves. On the other hand, in the social hierarchy systems we see perpetuated in schools nationwide, you can also become the target of every bully's joke. Othello became both things: an awkward leader and an oppressed mascot.

I want you to put yourself in Othello's shoes for a second: A young Black boy who lives in the housing projects across the street from his school. He is smart, so smart he remembers everything you can imagine about trains, his hobby of choice. He has also memorized where every train in New York City goes and can give you directions to just about anywhere you need to go. He has also been identified as a Special Education student. I always wondered why he was not identified as a gifted student, as well.

How often do you think about the needs of Special Education students? I want you to center them in your hearts and minds throughout this chapter. Think about your own experiences with students with special needs. I also want you to think about why Black and Brown boys are overrepresented in Special Education programs across the nation. What leadership policies and practices have led to the rise in these numbers? Finally, how can we embrace and realize a social justice approach to Special Education?

Chapter Objective

The purpose of this chapter is to name the direct connection between Special Education and social justice education (SJE) through my lived experiences and Critical Race Testimonies in the classroom as a New York City public school teacher. As such, student anecdotes in schooling spaces specifically, along with oppressive policies and practices that harm young people are viewed through my intersectional lenses with portraiture. By applying a phenomenological-based approach, portraiture is a research methodology that centers "context as crucial to the documentation of the human experience and organizational culture" (Lawrence-Lightfoot & Davis, 1997, p. 41). Therefore, I provide detailed observations of the schooling atmosphere surrounding the students and teachers. My vivid descriptions are used to set the scene since portraitists "view human experience as being framed and shaped by the setting" (Lawrence-Lightfoot & Davis, 1997, p. 41).

I also discuss the historical connections to Special Education through various policies such as the Individuals with Disabilities Education Act (IDEA), No Child Left Behind (NCLB), Jim Crow, and the 13th Amendment (along with its connections to the school-to-prison pipeline). Similarly, I touch on concepts such as neurodiversity and Collaborative Team

Teaching (CTT) to explore how Special Education shows up in various pedagogical contexts that are complex and does not adhere to a "one-size-fits-all" model. I argue that a lack of understanding of the diverse ways students learn and understand the world has also contributed to the overrepresentation of Black/Brown students in Special Education classrooms nationwide.

It is important to note that there is a teacher reflection and pedagogical activity placed in the middle of the chapter, to reinforce the idea that this work is non-linear and every chapter does not look the same, although all chapters are an exploration of the underlying question in the text: What exactly is SJE, in theory, and in practice? The pedagogical activity in this chapter (similar to the other activities) encourages self-reflection as a critical aspect of an SJE framework. The chapter also ends with takeaway questions as a way to reflect and prepare for a shift in pedagogical practices.

Last but certainly not least, most of the anecdotes and storytelling throughout this chapter intentionally focus on who I am as an activist, educator, and social justice advocate, naming the perils of racism and white supremacy, unapologetically, which undergirded my teaching career. These stories are rooted in Critical Race Theory (CRT) and are not meant to have simplistic beginning, middle, and endings. I often pause to share important details that help elevate the context surrounding the individual/location I am observing to remind you of the ways that physical environments and school culture(s) continuously impact the way teaching and learning happens.

Special Education, like antiracist and equity frameworks, is often at the end of planning agendas or to-do lists. I witnessed this as a teacher, professor, professional development specialist, and director of education. There is always an omission when it comes to Special Education as if simply acknowledging students with special needs is hard work. The inherent disproportionality that happens in Special Education across race and class is alarming, to say the least.

Special Education is critical to an SJE framework as it requires offering the full range of equitable resources to students who have disabilities. But in many schools across the nation, students with disabilities are physically ostracized from their peers, in basements, or in entirely different schools. Scholars and practitioners alike have underscored that "disability" itself is a culturally and socially constructed phenomenon. A Social Justice Education framework is inclusive and pushes against conceptions of what counts as "normal," which is really a coded word for adhering to a status quo that privileges cis-gendered and able-bodied students. For example, within an SJE framework, inclusivity in Special Education is experienced through a culture of high expectations, and integrated classrooms that include "mainstream students" and students with special needs instead of ostracizing students with special needs socially and academically, which typically happens in most schools.

In many of my schooling experiences growing up, Special Education students were often kept in the basement of the school building, literally below everyone else and we rarely, if ever, interacted with them. The silence around Special Education students was riddled with ignorance and inequality, a scary combination. Once I became an educator myself, my graduate teacher education provided me with a deeper knowledge of students who needed special assistance with cognitive, behavioral, physical, and/or emotional needs to meet the demands of the school curriculum. Thanks to great leadership, I learned that Special Education students learned best when they were included in "mainstream" classes in a CTT model, where a general education teacher is placed with a Special Education teacher to create more inclusive and social justice-oriented teaching and learning practices. I am grateful that my foundation as a teacher is based on this model, which only elevated my consciousness of social justice teaching and learning methods.

Because CRT, a legal theory, guides this educational testimony and counterstory, it is imperative to look at the ways the law acknowledges individuals with various disabilities starting with the American with Disabilities Act (ADA). Section 504 states:

> No qualified individual with a disability in the United States shall be excluded from, denied the benefits of, or be subjected to discrimination under any program or activity that either receives Federal financial assistance or is conducted by any Executive agency or the United States Postal Service.

Similarly, the IDEA requires public schools to make available to all eligible children with disabilities a free public education in the least restrictive environment that is appropriate to their individual needs. Although laws are in place for students with various disabilities, whether learning-based or physical, the enforcement of these laws varies from school to school, depending on both the overall school culture and the administrative commitment to SJE.

The Radical Love Note presented at the start of the chapter shared the story of one of my former students, Othello. Having Asperger's, Othello was a neurodiverse learner who deserved to be included in all aspects of teaching and learning. Neurodiversity refers to the idea that people experience the world in multiple ways depending on their respective identities and histories. The chart below, taken from neurodiversity advocate and writer Jillian Enright, provides an overview of terminology that is helpful for understanding how neurodiversity fits in with social justice teaching and learning practices. According to a recent article in the *Harvard Business Review*, "neurodiversity advocates encourage inclusive, nonjudgmental language" (Baumer & Freuh, 2021) as a way to provide access to multiple ways of knowing and being across various spaces (Figure 4.1).

FIGURE 4.1 ● Neurodiversity Terminology

Neurodiversity model	The natural diversity of human brains (biodiversity)
Neurodiversity paradigm	The philosophy of neurodiversity
Neurodiversity movement	The political and social justice movement
Neurodivergent	A person whose brain differs, or diverges, from the statistical norm
Neurotypical	A person whose brain does not differ from the statistical norm
Neurodiverse	A group of people with different types of brains

Source: Enright (2021).

When we think about Special Education, we need a common understanding of neurodiversity. Although Special Education was born out of the Civil Rights Movement, "too often other variables such as language, poverty, assessment practices, and lack of professional development and cultural competence support for teachers have played too big a role, resulting in unnecessary services or students learning in inappropriately restrictive environments" (Coates & Tresvant, 2016). When students do not receive the inclusive services they need, it hinders their educational progress. Similarly, when students are misclassified, it also hinders their ability to thrive in school and beyond. The question I want you to pause and ask yourself is this: How have you made space for neurodiversity in your classroom?

How have you made space for neurodiversity in your classroom?

Coined in the 1990s by journalist Harvey Blume and autism activist Judy Singer, the term neurodiversity explores neurological differences similar to other human differences such as race, gender identity, sexual orientation, etc. (Armstrong, 2017). The culture of *doing* school (the idea that school is a simple task of learning and repeating facts and information) often creates a strict learning environment with a one-size-fits-all approach that limits teachers' ability to cater to neurodivergent thinking and students with special needs. Quite often, the ignorance around neurodiversity and Special Education teaching and learning methods are rooted in fear and discrimination due to a history of educational policies that did more harm than good to many students, especially our most vulnerable student populations.

THE IMPACT OF FEAR ON EDUCATION

The beginning of my teaching career coincided with NCLB. NCLB was the prominent law for general education from 2002 to 2015 and schools were penalized if students did not perform well, namely on standardized test scores. The impact of NCLB hit me hard as a teacher because I was able to witness the deep and lasting impact it had on teachers and students.

For example, when I started my teaching career in East New York, Brooklyn, the city where I was born and raised, I immediately noticed the culture of fear that permeated the school building. It was the norm for my Assistant Principal at the time to walk into my classroom in the middle of my lesson and ask to see my lesson plan (as the students watched). I often felt dehumanized by this practice as it signified very little trust in teachers and an emotionally violent culture of "staying on your toes." Most teachers followed suit, so it was also hard to find colleagues who empathized with the ways that I was feeling.

I started writing my lesson plans for the entire week during the weekends, to give myself more time to breathe on a day-to-day basis. But that meant that I was working during the weekends when I might normally relax and re-energize. Because of overworking to meet the needs of the school culture and my students, I often felt exhausted as a teacher, making it hard to focus on what really mattered: my students' learning and the systems in place that were *supposed* to promote their learning. In truth, that system was about micromanaging teachers at all costs to ensure that test scores went up, even if only by a few points. Additionally, due to the impact of NCLB, students' grades were often changed without teachers' knowledge. This was done to make the school appear as though it was adhering to state guidelines. I learned this the hard way after the failing grade I provided to one student miraculously turned into a passing score as a way to keep students advancing to the next grade, regardless of whether they were academically ready or not.

Working within a culture of fear is the opposite of SJE. To practice being or becoming a social justice educator or to develop a social justice-oriented environment as a school leader, requires creating a culture of radical love and self-acceptance. The truth is, it is much harder to accept others when we have yet to accept ourselves. Part of the work I do with leaders through my background as a Self-care Coach (and the founder of an online coaching business, Self Love Life 101) in addition to being a scholar and educator, is facilitating deep investigations of the self to build awareness, as a way to leverage equitable outcomes for all students. Once we can look in the mirror and understand the nature of our lived experiences and biases, we can better work with our students by truly seeing them in all of their complexities, just as we are complex.

When a school culture of fear is replaced by a school culture of love and relational trust, leaders support teachers to lead students with an ethic of care and a pedagogy of love that centers academic rigor. Requiring intellectual depth from students comes from a space of love for their academic development and sustainable growth. In educator Zaretta Hammond's notable work, *Culturally Responsive Teaching and the Brain* (2014), she notes that "productive struggle" among students indicates a more independent approach to learning that leads to more ownership of one's academic journey. On the contrary, schools that operate from a culture of fear typically have low academic expectations for students (primarily Black and Brown students) because of the deficit thinking regarding student capabilities based on their lived experiences. Hammond notes that, "when operating from a deficit thinking paradigm, educators and policymakers believe that culturally and linguistically diverse students fail in schools because of their own deficiencies..." (p. 59). Thinking of students as deficient or lacking is not only the opposite of love, it is the very definition of oppression in the classroom since the same people who are responsible for supporting student learning are stuck in the confines of oppressive ideologies that see Black and Brown students as outside of the supposed educational "norm."

JIM CROW, THE 13TH AMENDMENT, AND SPECIAL EDUCATION

Historically speaking, there has been an overrepresentation of Black and Brown students in prisons and in Special Education classrooms. Research also shows that most prisoners have cognitive and emotional disabilities, drawing the connections among students with disabilities being set up on a pathway to prison. According to a report published in 2015 by the National Council on Disability, "studies show that up to 85 percent of youth in juvenile detention facilities have disabilities that make them eligible for Special Education services... A disproportionate percentage of these detained youth are youth of color."

Deficit mindsets about student capabilities are directly linked to the school-to-prison pipeline, which Michelle Alexander discusses in *The New Jim Crow: Mass Incarceration in the Age of Colorblindness* (2012). Essentially, low academic expectations are also linked to dependent learners which limits student potential and cognitive growth. Such a mindset creates young people who are being groomed for the prison system as opposed to the education system. Educator and author Zaretta Hammond analyzes Alexander's text and notes that,

> According to the Southern Poverty Law Center, the school-to-prison pipeline is a set of seemingly unconnected school policies and teacher instructional decisions that over time result in students of color not receiving adequate literacy and content instruction while being disproportionately disciplined for non-specific, subjective offenses such as "defiance." (Hammond, 2014, p. 13)

As highlighted in Hammond's interpretation of Alexander's work, the school-to-prison pipeline often begins with zero-tolerance policies that limit students' creative expression and sense of autonomy while enforcing strict disciplinary codes of conduct. Our schools have become sites of power, control, and dehumanization. Students' bodies seemingly belong to the security guards, the teachers, the administrators, and everybody except themselves. When you are no longer in control of your body, how is it that you are supposed to learn in a liberatory way? The control of bodies also has an eerie connection to chattel slavery, where Black bodies were literally controlled, dehumanized, and exploited for their labor. Think of Black/Brown student bodies as enemies of the state who are controlled through various systems of power such as schools and prisons.

Similar to Michelle Alexander's *New Jim Crow* book, film Director Ava Duvernay explores the impact of mass incarceration through the history of racial inequality in the United States in the documentary, *13th* (2016). Throughout the documentary,

Duvernay explores the impact of the prison industrial complex (PIC), which is how various businesses and organizations benefit from mass incarceration. The abolitionist organization, Critical Resistance, defines PIC "as a term to describe the overlapping interests of government and industry that use surveillance, policing, and imprisonment as solutions to economic, social and political problems" (Tufts University Prison Divestment, 2022). In fact, many prisoners create products for highly profitable organizations for free or cheap labor. Duvernay argues that the institution of slavery led to the perpetual exploitation of Black folx through prisons since Black folx make up a significant portion of the prison population. According to the Prison Policy Institute, Black people are disproportionately arrested and likely to be arrested again in the same year (2020). It is important to note the title refers to the 13th amendment in the United States Constitution, which states that, "Neither slavery nor involuntary servitude, except as a punishment for crime whereof the party shall have been duly convicted, shall exist within the United States, or any place subject to their jurisdiction." In other words, the 13th Amendment justifies slavery when it involves punishment of a crime, thereby highlighting the overarching theme in Alexander's book that the PIC echoes aspects of slavery, such as free labor and exploitation provided mostly by Black bodies.

It is no secret that our prison systems have an over-representation of Black people. Data from the Prison Policy Initiative notes that Black Americans currently make up 13% of the population. However, Black Americans represent 40% of the prison population. Similarly, it is hard to deny the current overrepresentation of Black folx in prisons along with the current overrepresentation of Black students in Special Education. According to the National Center for Learning Disabilities,

> Students of color, with the exception of Asian students, are identified for Special Education at a higher rate than their White peers. American Indian and Alaska Native children receive Special Education at twice the rate of the general student population, and Black students are 40 percent more likely to be identified with a disability versus all other students. (NCLD, 2020)

Black students are consistently overrepresented compared to other minority groups within Special Education, similar to how Black people are overrepresented within the PIC. Within the education system, there is a direct correlation between discipline and learning through the direct control of students' bodies. Public school education policies are quicker to align with compliance as opposed to equity and compassion, modeling a prison-style approach to teaching and learning.

As a middle- and high-school teacher, I witnessed firsthand how discipline was synonymous with control. It began from the moment you entered the building with metal detectors at the front door, where students were scanned and searched before starting their day. Students' sense of security was undermined by police officers present in the school building, dressed in full uniforms, so you often wondered if you were in a school or a prison. Along with a heavy police presence, zero-tolerance policies would automatically suspend students for getting into physical fights, and detention was regularly given for minor infractions like talking back, disrupting the teacher during a lesson, or having an argument with another student. Hallway passes were needed for going to the bathroom and students had to sign a logbook before leaving the classroom so that there was an ongoing record of who came and went into the classroom. As a teacher, these external forces made schools seem more like prisons, controlling students' bodies and minds, to supposedly provide a culture of safety, which was more so a culture of fear.

RADICAL LOVE REFLECTION: MY SPED STUDENTS WERE EVENTUALLY INCARCERATED

I am the teacher who has remained connected with my students long after I have taught them. These connections are mostly through social media and some are through phone calls and text messages over sixteen years later. I have seen many of my students go on to have children, complete their college education, attain Master's degrees, and get married. I have also noticed a pattern, particularly regarding my former Black male students who were in Special Education. Many of

(Continued)

(Continued)

them have ended up incarcerated often during or directly after high school. I started noticing this pattern a few years after I transitioned from teaching high-school students into an education doctoral program at Teachers College of Columbia University. The first time I noticed was when a student reached out to me on Facebook. When I went to check his page, I noticed that there were many messages from his friends saying, "free him," a common phrase used when Black men are incarcerated. He was only 18 years old at the time and wondered how I was doing, even though he was behind bars. I felt an immediate pang in my stomach, remembering all of the times I felt I was losing this young man in my classroom, due to a school culture that was more concerned about disciplining him than loving him.

The second (unfortunately not the last) time it occurred, was for a Black male student who struggled with behavioral issues in school, particularly when it came to sitting for long periods of time. Unlike the other young man, he was cared for and nurtured by teachers and our principal. His home life often conflicted with school due to various community pressures, which he wrote about extensively in his journal. He and I communicated regularly on Facebook, by liking one another's photos, commenting, and sending the occasional message. A couple of years out of high school, he seemed to be doing well. Until one day he was not, which I also learned on social media through tagged posts saying "free him."

It is no coincidence that young Black boys who become Black men, especially those who are in Special Education programs, are at risk of being incarcerated for a variety of reasons connected to systemic oppression and critical decision-making at certain times of their lives. Although these are two examples based on my own lived experience as an educator, unfortunately, I have several examples, and all are of Black men who were formerly in Special Education programs. I have continued to wonder, what we can do in schools on the backend, through social justice teaching and learning methods, to speak back to these direct connections to incarceration. A Social Justice Education framework intentionally disrupts the school-to-prison pipeline by naming it for students in school, so they can become more critically conscious and self-aware of the systems they are learning and living within while creating alternative pathways for growth and their ongoing freedom.

A social justice approach to teaching and learning is grounded in love. To teach is to love because it is a transference of knowledge that can then be adjusted to fit the other individual's level of understanding. To further emphasize this point, teaching is an intimate dance of deep observation, critical self-reflection, and radical love. It requires seeing someone fully and giving them the tools they need to learn and socialize as their authentic selves. The prison system is the opposite of love and is often rooted in brutality, oppression, and profit, as opposed to rehabilitation. The intersections between school systems and prisons are eerily similar, especially considering the high levels of mass shootings that have happened from Columbine, Colorado in 1999 to Sandy Hook, Connecticut in 2012 to Parkland, Florida in 2018 to Uvalde, Texas in 2022. When our schools become actual sites of terror coupled with anti-social justice teaching and learning strategies, it is safe to say that our humanity is in danger. Schools often serve as the cornerstone of the future, where children become adults and where adults refine ideas to help transform the world.

The question I want you to think about now is this: How can we embody a more reflective and reflexive teaching and learning process where love is at the center and not an afterthought, as is the case when fear dominates our decision-making and actions. I invite you to step into a pedagogical activity I call, *Mirror, Mirror*.

RADICAL LOVE ACTIVITY #4: MIRROR, MIRROR (SHADOW WORK)

This activity can be scaffolded for grades K-12

Learning Objective: Teachers and students will use mirrors as an act of self-reflection and community connection.

Radical Love Goal: In order for educators to develop deeper relationships with students, it is important for teachers and students to see one another as complex, multifaceted individuals with diverse lived experiences and cultural values.

The teacher will place students in mixed-ability groups to encourage diverse perspectives and lived experiences, not solely seating students based on academic ability. Each student will be provided with a mirror. Please ask students to bring a household mirror to school or ask the school administration to provide mirrors, if necessary for your school.

Total Activity Time = 45 minutes

(Continued)

(Continued)

Overview: The teacher/facilitator will explain the significance of shadow work. Students will begin by exploring shadows in their lives by engaging in dialogue using the following guiding questions:

1. How often do you think about your shadow? Explain using specific details connected to how you see yourself physically.

2. When you see your shadow, how does it make you feel?

3. In your opinion, does your shadow accurately portray your body? Why or why not?

Activity #1—Shadow Work: Each student will be instructed to look in the mirror for a couple of minutes in silence, at their respective tables. The students will examine their physical selves while reflecting on the guided questions. Students will be given 10–15 minutes of independent time to create a first-person journal style entry, based on what came up while doing their shadow work, as they looked in the mirror. Teachers should encourage students to be honest about how they see themselves by participating in the activity with them and being vulnerable in their responses, as well. Teachers should be prepared for responses that may be racially-sensitive or emotionally charged. Be prepared to offer students additional support in the form of school counseling afterward, if needed. This portion of the activity should last 20 minutes.

Activity #2—Think-Pair-Share: Students will explore the guiding questions more intentionally by doing a Think-Pair-Share, a collaborative teaching and learning strategy, where students work together to have critical discussions and/or solve problems in the process. Students will work with a partner to reflect on the guiding questions. A Think-Pair-Share is a teaching strategy that encourages individual thinking, collaboration, and a presentation in the same activity. First, students respond to a prompt on their own, then come together and share with a partner. Finally, students will share with the entire group, to cement what they have learned during the process.

An example of a Think-Pair-Share with the Shadow Work Activity would include:

1. Students will respond to one of the guided questions provided.

2. Students will share with a partner their respective thoughts about the particular question.

3. Students will present their individual responses that they have had time to process on their own and discuss with a partner with the larger group.

This portion of the activity should last 10 minutes.

Activity #3—Whole Group Share: The entire class will come together to share their shadow work journal entries. The teacher should request a volunteer from each table to ensure a diverse representation of voices and lived experiences. This portion of the activity should last 15 minutes.

PEDAGOGICAL REFLECTION

Shadow work is an exercise I use in my coaching practice, through my radical self-care coaching and consulting business, Self Love Life 101 (selflovelife101.com). The purpose of shadow work is to reveal some of our own struggles with how we see ourselves and how that impacts how we see others while navigating the highs and lows of life. I guide clients through the necessary steps of shadow work, by having them reflect on who they see in the mirror and how that is directly connected to social constructions of race, class, gender, ability, and sexuality. The overall goal is to help them unpack the shadows that hide within us because we are afraid of our own individual complexities, which we all have. Understanding our individual complexities through our various identities will allow us to love ourselves more which in turn, allows us to love others more, as well.

As a secondary English teacher, I used shadow work often with my students, since I realized that assisting students with building up their self-esteem was just as important as teaching the curriculum or preparing them for standardized exams. How a student sees themselves, especially in relation to large organizational systems like schools, is critical for their development as unique individuals in this world.

My approach to shadow work is guided by a culturally responsive paradigm, which honored the lived experiences of my students as a critical component of the curriculum. For example, every day in my classroom, students had opportunities to reflect on various events happening in their communities and respective lives. Sample journal prompts to bridge students' lives with the school curriculum included:

- Describe something you witnessed recently in your community that was memorable.

- How long have you lived in your neighborhood? Do you feel connected to where you live? Explain.

- What is a holiday that your family celebrates? How do you feel about this holiday and why?

- Think about a time when you were the only person with a particular characteristic in a room (only boy, only girl, only person wearing glasses, etc.). Did you experience any discomfort? Write about your experience.

It is imperative that we build bridges between home and school since "teachers need to know about the lives of the *specific children* they teach" (Villegas & Lucas, 2002, p. 80). When we honor who students are, we give them the space to be and to become their authentic selves, which is the true sense of urgency we need. As noted in scholar Dr. Gholdy Muhammad's book, *Cultivating Genius: An Equity Framework for Culturally and Historically Responsive Literacy* (2020): "We live in a period where there's no time for 'urgent-free' pedagogy. Our instructional pursuits must be honest, bold, raw, unapologetic, and responsive to the social times" (p. 54). My shadow work exercises are a direct example of a social justice and radical self-care pedagogy that is responsive to these challenging times we find ourselves in, with the lingering effects of COVID-19 still present in our communities and schools over three years later.

SUPPORTIVE LEADERS MAKE SPACE FOR SJE

I was able to effectively model culturally responsive teaching and learning practices with the support of Mr. Lovejoy, principal of the Brooklyn Love School (BLS), during my tenure as a High-School English teacher. Mr. Lovejoy taught me a lot about what it means to break down the hierarchy in school systems that were traditionally sites of oppression. He also advocated for Special Education not as an afterthought, but at the center of our teaching and learning practices, which embodies SJE. Some days, Mr. Lovejoy and I had the best relationship, bouncing ideas off of one another and giving me space to hone in on masterful lesson planning. Some days, we did not get along, due to me not following school procedures I believed were harmful and oppressive. For example, when students wanted to use the bathroom, I just let them go because it is a basic human right. And sometimes a student is just bored and wants to walk around. So what? I hated the idea of giving students a "hall pass" to justify their reason for walking in their own school and most importantly, to go to the restroom. Most of the time, my students left and returned without incident. However, there were a few times when they encountered the dean or Mr. Lovejoy. The students would be returned to me with a stern *where is their pass* questioning, to which I always responded: "Using the bathroom is a basic human right." Although he did not agree at first, Mr. Lovejoy did not penalize me and I was labeled as a kind of *good* troublemaker, but a troublemaker, nonetheless. Although we did not agree on everything, Mr. Lovejoy understood what I was doing and made space for me to practice these social justice methods I was in the process of formulating as a teacher.

When I think of the connections between culturally responsive education, Special Education, social justice, and its impact on the lives of students, I am reminded of Jeffrey, a student I taught at the BLS, who was deeply misunderstood, due to his shyness. As a result, he was perceived as a student with special needs. Jeffrey's educational trajectory, as you will soon learn, was deeply impacted by the mindsets and behaviors of the teachers around him. This is also connected to the ways that Black boys are overrepresented in Special Education, due to a misdiagnosis of who they are, based on some teachers' stereotypical percep-tions of who they are cognitively, socially, and emotionally.

JEFFREY AND THE BROOKLYN LOVE SCHOOL

There are particular students who stand out when it comes to my shadow work and inclusivity in the classroom, especially when it comes to Special Education and social justice. The first student, whom I will call Jeffrey, was a ninth-grade student in my English classroom back in Bedford-Stuyvesant, Brooklyn (Bed-Stuy) at BLS. Unlike the first school I taught at in East New York, BLS was committed to social justice teaching and learning practices and our CTT model ensured that Special Education students and "general" education students were learning together in the same classrooms with a certified Special Education teacher and a content-certified teacher, depending on the particular subject. This pushed every teacher to reimagine their teaching practices by intentionally becoming more inclusive and welcoming of students with special needs and neurodivergence.

Jeffrey had light caramel skin, calm eyes, and a warm demeanor. He was the kind of student who intentionally wanted to be in the background, a true introverted personality based on my observations. He was also very respectful and would only speak if asked a question or asked to participate in partner or group work. Immediately, Jeffrey defied stereotypical tropes of the average Black male youth. I had come to learn that some of my own biases about Black boys in Brooklyn, based on my personal experiences as a sister of Black boys and lover of Black men, had to be unlearned if I wanted to be an effective social justice educator to students like Jeffrey and those unlike him, too. Jeffrey happened to live in the community that surrounded the school, just a few short blocks away. He never missed a day of school. If a high-school student shows up to school daily and on time, there is usually an ethic of care in his life with regard to discipline and structure. Of course, this is not always the case, but I want to share some of my own biases about how I see and come to know students.

Jeffrey was also very driven by creativity and thrived in his art classes. I knew this because I often communicated with his other teachers. As social justice educators, when we talk to other teachers about the students we teach through a radical self-care lens, we gain much more insight into who they are inside and outside of our classrooms. Speaking to other teachers about the self-care and holistic growth of our students also helps build a radical professional community, which encourages everyone to lead with compassion and equity.

"SHOULD WE RECOMMEND HIM FOR SPECIAL ED?" JEFFREY AND THE SHADOW OF MS. BLOOM

It had been six months since I started working at BLS and I was feeling a deep culture of belonging due to the support of the administration and the innovation of the other teachers, whom I continued to learn a lot from. We did not always get along and we certainly were not always singing *kumbaya*. However, we all had mutual respect and certainly knew how to work together regardless of our teaching styles, which was a direct manifestation of the principal's vision for developing and sustaining professional learning communities (PLCs) in schools. To illustrate this point further, every Wednesday we had professional development by creating a schedule where we had longer class periods to maximize student learning time throughout the week. Therefore, the extra student learning time allowed us to carve out space for Professional Development Wednesdays, where students also had a half day of school. This particular schedule still adhered to state mandates for student learning hours per week throughout the school year. Setting aside intentional time for professional learning that is genuinely grounded in self-care and teacher collaboration, and self-reflection was the first time in my teaching career I experienced a model of SJE. My voice mattered, my opinions about my students mattered and relational trust was at the heart of it all. These key ingredients were essential components of the school culture at BLS.

One day after school, on a Professional Development Wednesday, we were sitting in a teacher named Ms. Bloom's classroom, where we had our weekly grade-team meetings. It should be noted that during these meetings, Special Education teachers and general education teachers worked together since we all taught in mixed classrooms. During grade-team meetings, all ninth-grade teachers (the team I was a part of at the time), would sit and share "glows" and "grows" about students. A "glow" is something positive the student is doing academically or behaviorally to ensure their success. A "grow" is something students may be struggling with and need more support with moving forward. This space served as an interdisciplinary ongoing grade-team PLC.

Ms. Bloom was unpopular with most students and faculty. She often came across as brash and disrespectful if you did not agree with her teaching methods. Understanding Ms. Bloom's background as a white middle-class high-school teacher originally from New England is important to this upcoming narrative as it pertains to Jeffrey. You see, unlike Ms. Bloom, Jeffrey was an immigrant, having come to the United States just a few years beforehand, from a small Caribbean island. Although English is the national language there, education operates differently in the Caribbean, so our system in the US was foreign to what Jeffrey knew. I suspect this is another reason why he was so quiet: he was still trying to find his footing as a young teenager in a new country and within a new school system. I am not sure that Ms. Bloom knew this or cared to know. How did I know? I spoke to Jeffrey's mother, as I made welcoming phone calls to all of my parents at the beginning of the school year and thereafter to build community and radical trust. My *just because phone calls* were one way I could show parents that I cared about more than their children's academic performance (although that was important, too)! I also cared about who they were and aspiring to become. I cared about their hopes, dreams, and fears. I cared about their favorite food and musical interests. To know someone is to understand their strengths, struggles, flaws, and frustrations. To fully love our students in a radical love and self-care-driven way, requires us to really *know* them outside of academic data. Unlike the culture of *doing* school, this model is based on social justice and understanding.

To fully love our students in a radical love and self-care driven way, requires us to really know *them outside of academic data.*

Having grade-team meetings with Ms. Bloom became such a challenge that I would always bring papers to grade, as a way to protect my energy from her racially coded and judgmental language. For example, she often used the terms "these students" or "these kids" when referring to our predominantly Black and Brown students. She never referred to the few white or Asian students we had at our school in this manner. She also referred to Black boys as "bad" often to their faces and also during meetings. I also challenged her when I had the emotional and mental energy to deal with what I call *Karen Racism*. Karen has become a name associated with white women who call the police on Black people for no reason. At the time I was working with Ms. Bloom, "Karen" had not yet come to light as a phenomenon, however, the attitudes and behaviors associated with the name had existed long before the term. *Karen Racism* is when white women intentionally use their positions of power to uphold white supremacy at the expense of Black, Indigenous, and people of color (BIPOC) communities, but especially, Black communities, usually by unjustly calling the police on Black people. The reason why the term *Karen* became popular to call out white women using their power to particularly harm Black communities, derived from public instances that went viral in the media. One example was when a Black man named Christian Cooper, was bird watching in Central Park in a leashed dog area. A white woman in the park had an unleashed dog and he asked her to put her dog on a leash. The white woman, whose name is Amy Cooper, proceeded to call the police, claiming that he was threatening her life. Thankfully, he was recording the entire video, which went viral, proving he did nothing wrong. There are more examples of white women calling the police on Black people who are doing ordinary things like bird watching or having a barbecue. It speaks to the deep racial tension in our nation and the importance of naming how white supremacy continues to put many Black people in danger, especially in a country where many Black people have died at the hands of police, as noted at the beginning of this book. Being a social justice educator requires us to call out and push against racial injustices we see in schools, which are representations of what is happening throughout society.

Ms. Bloom was the original Karen in my life throughout my teaching career, although many came before and after her, unfortunately. She also lived in the surrounding community in one of the more expensive brownstones that were going for $1700 a month for a studio at that time (this was considered expensive in 2009). There were rumors she lived in a two-bedroom with her partner and that they owned the property. Understanding all of the ways that Ms. Bloom used her **whiteness as property,** a CRT theory that draws on how white identity is connected to conceptions of value and power (Harris, 2011), is very important in relation to the use of portraiture while offering deeper contextual aspects of Jeffrey's story.

We were sitting in Ms. Bloom's classroom. It was the fall, which I remember because the students were writing first-person narratives, which was always my first unit at the beginning of the school year. I began with their narratives to center the student's voices in their writing (a culturally relevant teaching and learning strategy). The writing would then be published into a full book which would be used as an ongoing curriculum for future freshman classes. Mr. Lovejoy put that brilliant idea in motion and it worked wonders for student engagement in my classroom.

On that particular Wednesday afternoon in Ms. Bloom's classroom, filled with large pothos plants and buckets of yarn (she ran a knitting club that was very popular, which gave me pause about some of my own assumptions about her *Karen* behaviors), we were discussing which students needed an *intervention*, which was a restorative justice behavioral approach to students who were underperforming academically and struggling socially. If you are not familiar with the concept of restorative justice in schools, it refers to alternative methods of disciplining students in a way that provides them with ownership of their choices, while making spaces for self-reflection and ultimately self-improvement. A popular example of this practice is when the Maryland State Department of Education (MSDE) implemented a restorative justice policy in 2019 that offered, for example, yoga for students instead of detention. The implementation of this restorative justice policy led to higher student academic outcomes while helping to lower suspension rates, especially for Black students.

So you may be wondering what this has to do with Jeffrey. Well, as we were discussing students who needed these restorative justice style interventions, Ms. Bloom suddenly paused the meeting to announce that she had a *major* concern with one student we had not mentioned: Jeffrey. Everyone paused, almost as if in a trance because Jeffrey was certainly a student who did not need this kind of intervention, especially since he had no academic or behavioral issues. I stopped pretending to grade first-person narratives and looked around to read the temperature of the room. Jefferey was a relatively quiet student who had mostly Bs and a few Cs. As a high-school freshman, this was not considered outside of the *norm*. But as Karens often do, once they introduce an idea about a [Black] student or about anything pertaining to teaching and learning in a school setting, everybody listens, almost instantly.

Ms. Bloom was wearing a white silk blouse that hung loosely over her slender, muscular body. She then stood up and said confidently, "He seems really quiet and I was wondering if we should recommend him for Special Ed?" Ms. Bloom did not mention anything about Jeffrey's personality, his academic and social experiences in her ninth-grade Earth Science class (which students kept complaining about), or why his "quiet" demeanor was considered problematic. Everyone remained silent and I knew that this was an opportunity for me to shed more light on who Jeffrey was based on my experiences as his English teacher. I cleared my throat and said: "Jeffrey is doing pretty well in my class and is currently earning a B+. He is a quiet boy, which does not mean that he has special needs." Ms. Bloom looked at me sternly, like I was one of the Black male students she constantly yelled at in her classroom, in the hallway, and even in the lunchroom when she was occasionally given lunch duty. Her *Karen-isms* were all over the school building by the way she treated BIPOC students as well as BIPOC teachers and I could not sit this one out, knowing the implications it could have upon Jeffrey's life as a young Black boy in a public high school.

"He seems really quiet and I was wondering if we should recommend him for Special Ed?"

An uneasy tension permeated the classroom air which already smelled like soil, oversized plants, and mason jar salads, which Ms. Bloom ate often during our grade-team meetings. One thing that stood out, glaringly so: every other white teacher in the space was silent and would not advocate for Jeffrey. Rather, they were all willing to take Ms. Bloom's word for it, which emphasizes the power that white teachers have in schools that serve predominantly Black/Brown students. I do not believe that they did not agree with me, because I spoke to many of them outside of that meeting, rather, they too, were fearful of Ms. Bloom. At the time, I was the sole Black ninth-grade team teacher and the only one making a case for us to fully *see* Jeffrey, not only what our biases would have us believe about him. Jeffrey was an artist, and a recent Caribbean immigrant, who was new to the United States. His personality was more introverted. These were characteristics that Ms. Bloom was oblivious to because she did not get to know her students on a deeper level, beyond their test scores. Imagine being labeled as a student with special needs, solely because you did not fit into a stereotypical conception of who someone (your teacher in a position of power) thought you were. This is how white supremacy remains intact. When white educators do not take a stand against the structural violence toward BIPOC students in classrooms, especially, when it comes to the overrepresentation of Black boys in Special Education, they are not only perpetuating racist status quos, but they are also forever impacting the lives of young boys like Jeffrey and others like him, who fit into non-traditional conceptions of who Black boys are, can be and become.

Jeffrey went on to do well at BLS and become very active in art and filmmaking, a passion of his. He was always an introverted student and continued to express himself in the ways that felt most safe to him in a new school and a new country. I followed Jeffrey's journey long after I taught him and I remember when he graduated from college (which I learned through a Facebook update). A single tear rolled down my right cheek, as I remembered that fateful day in Ms. Bloom's classroom when I had to advocate for his inclusion to just *be* who he was due to a *Karen* in a position of power who did not take the time to know him *fully*, only stereotypically, based on her own assumptions about who young Black boys in Bed-Stuy were. To be clear, Special Education is an important aspect of SJE, creating more inclusive spaces for differentiated learning styles and experiences. If Jeffrey did need additional learning services that are part of having an Individualized Education Plan (IEP) I would have advocated for that, too. Many of our students did, in fact, have IEPs and thrived with our culturally responsive and social justice-aligned teaching and learning models. The point is, that is not what Jeffrey needed at the time and someone had to be a voice for him in a room where he could not make decisions.

I wish I could say that Jeffrey's story has been rare throughout my career. However, I see this happen often, the desire to put Black boys in alternative learning spaces because there is a perception that something is *wrong* or they do not *fit the mold* of doing school. A Social Justice Education framework requires us to unlearn our biases in order to be the best version of ourselves. Becoming the best version of ourselves as educators incorporates the process of doing the inner shadow work, that helps us see our strengths and weaknesses clearly. As a result, we will make better decisions for our students in the classroom.

It is imperative that we learn more about the community surrounding BLS and how I ended up there in the first place, to further understand Jeffrey as an individual and my ability to share some of his story with you today. These relationships are like fractal images of the kind of love and care students need: respect for and interest in diversity, room for wisdom and information from unexpected sources, and the centrality of relationships and understanding for effective and equitable teaching. This pause is intentional, as a way to decenter linear education narratives that easily go from point A to point B. As a portraitist, operating under a portraiture framework, through CRT, this is an intentional counterstory (a tool used by BIPOC to tell stories that reflect their experiences and knowledge), that pushes against traditional conceptions of how narratives are written. As noted in Sara Lawrence-Lightfoot's text, *The Art and Science of Portraiture* (1997), "this process of creating the narrative requires a difficult (sometimes paradoxical) vigilance to empirical description *and* aesthetic expression. It is a careful deliberative process and a highly creative one" (p. 12).

Let me introduce you to Bed-Stuy. If you have never been there, think of tree-lined streets with gorgeous Victorian-style brownstones, *bodegas*[1] on every other corner, mostly Black and

---

[1]The word bodega is derived from the Spanish word "storeroom" or "wine cellar." In urban communities, a bodega refers to a small convenience store that also serves hot food.

Brown children playing and going to school, and of course your urban community doses of liquor stores and high-rise buildings, in the form of housing projects and condominiums. The streets talk, and from block to block you can hear the sound of newborn babies crying and cooing, the hustlers playing craps[2] on various corners, someone speaking Spanish or Spanglish, police sirens zooming by, and ambulances not too far off in the distance. Bed-Stuy always has a vibrant noise, a particular charm that embraces its origin story as a major cultural center for Brooklyn's African-American population.

BLS is situated in the section of Bed-Stuy that is bordered by Flushing Avenue to the north (bordering Williamsburg), Classon Avenue to the west (bordering Clinton Hill), Broadway to the east (bordering Bushwick and East New York) and Atlantic Avenue to the south (bordering Crown Heights and Brownsville). It should be noted that the school, like many schools in New York City, is housed in a large old public school building that also houses two charter schools in addition to BLS, which is not a charter school. BLS was able to occupy space in that building because the previous school (named after a Founding Father at that…) was closed in 2008 due to "low student achievement and unruly student behavior" according to Inside Schools, a private consulting organization that provides insider information about New York City public school sites. The reviews are actually written by journalists who spend time visiting the schools and talking to parents, students, teachers, and administration. In essence, BLS was launched in the space of a former traditional public school that was deemed a *failure*, in the eyes of the state and according to standardized testing. In the context of social justice, this is a prime example of the ways that capitalism forces us to fight for resources, consistently creating a scarcity mindset, which is designed to exploit all workers by keeping them in a perpetual state of, *there is not enough for everyone, so be lucky you have anything at all.* In order for BLS to exist, a previous school had to fail. It was impossible for both schools to coexist.

---

[2]Craps is a street term for shooting dice. It is a gambling game where one person throws the dice and other players bet on what the number will be.

I remember the first day I arrived at the school for an interview. It was a relatively warm day in April of 2008, about 65 degrees. I remember because I was wearing my favorite brown bomber leather jacket I had recently purchased from the Target located near the Flatbush Nostrand Junction.[3] My chin-length locs touched the top of my neck and I was wearing my favorite (and only) black suit that I had purchased in my junior year of college for all job interviews and internships. At that point, the Anne Taylor suit held up well, especially after five years, making its rounds in every interview. My West-Indian mother always stressed the importance of "*havin' ah good black suit!*" While adorning my worn-in black suit, a confident attitude and excitement in my spirit, I approached the large brick-style elementary school building that was the exact structure of my own elementary school in the North Flatbush section of Brooklyn. It was at that moment when I thought to myself, *all the schools seem to be constructed the same way, too many bricks, not enough greenery.* But because of my personal history with buildings like this, I thought to myself, *I already know what to expect when I walk inside,* and that turned out to be true.

I had taken the day off to visit BLS. At the time, I was in my second year of teaching at another school in East New York, Brooklyn, where I felt oppressed as a teacher with very little autonomy and a school culture of control. My desire to create more liberation in the classroom through culturally responsive lessons and social justice-inspired themes bothered the administration and the toxic leadership style was demoralizing early on in my teaching career. I had to make a change for myself if I had any plans of remaining in the teaching profession and this interview was the first step toward my own liberation as a relatively new teacher.

Upon walking into the seemingly familiar building, I was immediately approached by about ten to twelve steps that led up to a security desk, *just like most of the New York City Public*

---

[3]The Flatbush Nostrand Junction is an area in Brooklyn, NY located at the intersections of Flatbush and Nostrand Avenues, respectively. It is commonly referred to as "The Junction" and features several local and commercial shopping centers.

Schools I had entered over the years as a student, teacher, and job candidate. The straight wide steps were gray and appeared to be recently mopped by the way it shined: just enough to look clean without being too shiny to cause a slippery accident. When I got to the top of the steps, the security officer smiled kindly and said: "Hello, good afternoon. How may I help you?" She was a large, chestnut-colored Black woman with warm eyes, and long cornrow braids that draped her back. With flawless skin and no makeup, she was an all-natural stunner with minimal effort. Her security uniform was similar to the New York Police Department (NYPD) since at the time, School Safety Agents (SSAs) were housed under the supervision of the NYPD as opposed to the Department of Education. A living, breathing example of the school-to-prison pipeline in full view. However, admittedly, at the time, I did not yet have the language that I have now. Therefore, at that moment, all I knew was that this sista was kind and extended a generous smile toward my way, as I signed the check-in book with details like name, address, and photo identification before I was able to head upstairs to the interview room. Yet still, seeing a SSA in attire that resembled police shook me up, just a little bit, even as a Brooklyn public school native. The SSA, whom I will call Martha, turned out to be one of my most trusted allies in the building. We learned to rely on one another through the ups and downs of high-school student drama in a New York City public school context. She broke up many fights with that warm face and those *very* strong hands. Martha was a critical component of school safety, as students would automatically try to reconsider their choices, once they saw her disapproving face coming near them whenever an incident occurred.

The SSAs are not only in schools to *honor and protect* but also to build relationships with teachers, students, faculty, staff, and administration. Quite often, SSAs have the most diverse information in the building about what's happening where, and why. When we are able to see everyone as equally valuable contributors in any organizational chart and within large systems like public education, we can begin to disrupt hierarchy, which helps to create more spaces for individual and community liberation, respectively.

I was eventually offered the job and BLS became the school where I was able to experience the autonomy to step into who I was and still am, as a teacher, without having to compromise my various identities or cultural ways of knowing and being. At my previous school, I had to "fall in line" and never question the administration, which did not adhere to my social justice ways of knowing, being, and becoming. Special Education students were also treated as inferior at my previous school and were separated from the general population at all times. At BLS, it was not public knowledge that students were in Special Education unless you were a teacher, which gave those students a sense of academic and social liberation that positively impacted their in-school experiences among teachers and their peers. An SJE way of knowing encourages us to see everyone as a critical community member within any organization, and that goes for students with special needs as well as students outside of that distinction, as well.

Throughout this chapter, I have taken you on a journey that details the connections between Special Education and a Social Justice Education framework. There are systems within public schools that mirror the school-to-prison pipeline and the overrepresentation of Black boys in Special Education, similar to the ways that our society maintains laws that intentionally harm our most underserved and vulnerable populations inside and outside of school. It is imperative that we understand that inclusivity in education must honor Special Education as a range of services to assist and support students with diverse cognitive, emotional, and social needs.

Due to the negative label that Special Education has received due to educational disparities, racism, and teachers who are not adequately prepared to teach them in holistic and radically loving ways, we must start with ourselves, by understanding who students are as individuals, as learners and as critical thinkers with much to offer in the classroom, once we develop the environment for them to do so. I want you to reflect on the following questions below as a takeaway from this chapter:

- How will you center neurodivergent learning as a social justice teaching and learning practice moving forward?

- Who are you willing to stand up to in order to advocate for students with special needs?

- In what ways will you foster student inclusivity through diverse teaching and learning methods using an SJE framework? (Ex: talking to students' parents/guardians to learn more about them on an ongoing basis, providing more surveys where students provide feedback on your teaching and allowing students to bring their authentic selves to school.)

Radical love is at the center of reimagining Special Education practices that are more humanizing and less oppressive. We have to intentionally love our students in order to fully *see* them. I want you to remember how this chapter began, with the story of Othello, a student who was, in fact, a student with special needs who suffered socially because other students were not prepared to deal with someone who appeared to be outside of the *norm* they were accustomed to, leading to emotional trauma throughout his high-school career. Even though many teachers tried to cultivate more spaces of belonging for Othello in school, which worked sometimes, the ostracism he faced outside of school only compounded how difficult a task we had upon us. Therefore, SJE also requires us to think about strategic ways to better serve the communities that we teach in, as well. How often do we invite the surrounding community into the school community to learn something new? To take a free workshop or a job training? To understand different themes about diversity, equity, and inclusion? We can work to build these frameworks into the school community so that we are not only teaching inside but thinking about how we are impacting the surrounding school environment and people, as well.

Remember that Special Education teaching is a social justice enterprise because it demands self-care and radical love for our students. It requires us to see them *fully*, unlike the way Ms. Bloom could not see Jeffrey, due to her own biases. We all have biases that can limit the ways we teach and lead. Being self-reflective about our biases and educating ourselves on the history of Special Education in this country and how it is directly connected to various systems of oppression can allow us to lead with more love, light, and liberation.

CHAPTER 5

From the Mouths of Social Justice Educators

We all know the truth: More connects us than separates us. But in times of crisis, the wise build bridges, while the foolish build barriers.
(Black Panther, "Black Panther")

RADICAL LOVE NOTE #5

Our collective humanity is a swinging pendulum of our faith in one another. Faith is believing in what we have yet to see or have only witnessed in momentary bursts. Many times, this is experienced in the classroom. Like that magical moment when a student who has been struggling with a concept finally arrives at a clear understanding. Or that complex moment when you learn to collaborate with a colleague who has a completely different approach to teaching and learning.

I became a better teacher when I learned about the art of collaborative team teaching (CTT). CTT was introduced to me by one of my favorite school leaders at Brooklyn Love School. A class that is co-taught is one in which a "general" education teacher and a Special Education teacher work together to meet the needs of students with various learning styles. Equitable learning environments are created because students with diverse ways of learning and understanding share space and, most importantly, learn from one another. At first, I was resistant to the idea, stuck in the ways of wanting to do everything myself, which is opposed to the social justice approach of teaching and learning. But then I met Mr. Lombardo in 2009, my third year of teaching. Mr. Lombardo was a tall, thin white man with blond hair, a huge heart, and a powerful way of engaging the most complex students in the learning process of our collaborative English class.

On the surface, Mr. Lombardo and I were very different. He is white; I am Black. He was certified in Special Education; I was certified to teach English Language Arts. He had a calm approach to teaching and learning; I had a deep sense of urgency in my approach due to my lived experiences as a Black teacher who used to be a Black girl in similar Brooklyn class-rooms back in the day. Both of our approaches mattered to our students and to ourselves, but it was not until we learned to radically love and respect one another that our teaching dynamic was able to have a transformative impact on our students.

Over time, Mr. Lombardo and I developed a synergy where we understood one another's strengths and weaknesses. We had warm moments, tense moments when we disagreed on how to teach something to a diverse group of learners, and absolutely transformative moments where we both led our students to academic success in the classroom. This relationship between Mr. Lombardo and I took a few years to cultivate. The trust, the truth, and the transparency did not happen overnight. It happened over a series of radical love experiences in the classroom. In the following chapter, I will introduce you to social justice educators who learned more about themselves as teachers through a radical love for centering equity in the classroom. Their commitment to social justice teaching and learning practices helped them transform in various ways.

Chapter Objective

The purpose of this chapter is to invite you into a conversation that is not typical of your standard education research narratives. Instead, this chapter takes you on a journey into the minds and hearts of individuals who self-identify as social justice educators based on how they teach and how they create spaces of freedom for their students. The research is presented in a conversational approach to the ongoing question being answered throughout the book, *What is social justice education?*

I first introduce you to each participant and these introductions are my biased understandings of who they are based on how I know them (professionally, in a college context, or through the parameters of this small sample size study). My words are italicized and their words are in regular font as a way to note the distinction between their words and my own. This intentional dance between the researcher and participants is meant to reflect our connections, disconnections, similarities, differences, and various understandings of social justice education. I am also interpreting their words based on my lenses as a portraitist and Critical Race Theorist committed to teaching and learning practices grounded in radical love. The goal is not to judge them per se, but to offer the reader an understanding of how I interpret their words and how they fit into the larger themes of the book regarding education, social justice, and radical love. As Lawrence-Lightfoot and Davis (1997) discuss, "it is not only important for the portraitist to paint the contours and dimensions of the setting, it is also crucial that she sketch herself into the context. The researcher is the stranger, the newcomer, the interloper-entering the place and engaging the people, and disturbing the natural rhythms of the environment" (p. 50). I also provide what I call Radical Love Reflections (RLRs) for each participant, which is a personal response to them that acknowledges their words and ideas while reminding the reader that this work is always committed to radical love, deep reflection, and social justice.

Portraiture as a research framework intentionally pushes against traditional conceptions of how research is presented, particularly in education research. As a method, portraiture disrupts the status quo and hierarchical conceptions of how research can be presented in an academic book. As you read the words of the educators/participants, I want you to envision how you can use portraiture as a tool to gain a deeper understanding of various aspects of your school culture that may be harmful to the students you are teaching and/or to the teachers you are leading. I encourage you to continue to open your hearts and your perceptions (misconceptions, too) as you embark on these words.

At the end of the chapter, I also offer five key strategies you can implement in your classroom immediately, which were inspired by the courage, the words, and the testimonies of my participants. I am grateful for the ways that their voices speak to one another as well as challenge one another based on their own identities and lived experiences across race, class, and gender.

EMERGENT STRATEGIES AND SOCIAL JUSTICE EDUCATION THROUGH CRT AND PORTRAITURE

Strategies and routines are an important aspect of how we all function on a day-to-day basis. Developing strategies generally requires working collaboratively to organize various systems that serve multiple people. Strategies can be as simple as crossing the street or as complex as creating viral content on social media. I want you to pause and think about this for a second. When you cross the street, you typically stop and look both ways to ensure there are no cars coming. Or, if you are old-school, you wait until the light turns red before crossing. In fact, the first lesson that my caramel-colored, Trini-accent-speaking Black mother ever taught me about walking to elementary school alone was: "Make sure di light is red before you cross!" Those words meant everything to me up until the age I learned that even if the light was not red if no cars were on the street, I could also cross safely. In this situation, I revised the original strategy to suit my evolving needs as a pedestrian.

Now let's consider the complex scenario: going viral on social media. For the purposes of transparency and truth-telling, two critical social justice ingredients, I have never had any of my posts go viral on social media. However, I have created and read hundreds of thousands of social media posts at this point. Therefore, I have a clear idea of the kinds of posts that go viral: something that causes extreme joy or something that is provocative enough to create multiple reactions across a range of emotions. There are many social media strategies for going viral. Some people use the "make people laugh" formula and it works instantly. Some use personal testimonies. Others use the same formulas, and it takes years of effort to see results. Unlike crossing the street, going viral on social media isn't the product of a single strategy. Rather, there are multiple approaches, and which is successful often depends on further factors, like the number of followers the content creator has and the level of exposure the post receives.

This chapter presents a third kind of strategy in relation to education: an emergent one. What makes a strategy emergent? In

Adrienne Maree Brown's seminal text, *Emergent Strategy: Shaping Change, Changing Worlds* (2017), the author describes *emergence* as "the way complex systems and patterns arise out of a multiplicity of relatively simple interactions" (Brown, p. 3). I want you to pause and think about the simple things you do each day like brushing your teeth, getting dressed, checking the weather on your phone, and so on. Many of these habits are so embedded in your consciousness that you no longer have to think about doing them. Similarly, my re-imagination of education requires us to adopt a Social Justice Education framework so that its emergent strategies come to us as readily as the simple ones, like checking an app or crossing the street.

Imagine that kind of critical intentionality in your day-to-day lives. Throughout the following pages, you will meet five individuals, each with a different background in education that is ultimately connected by a common thread: social justice education teaching and learning practices. As you encounter the complexity of their experiences and voices, I will weave in creative and poetic observations (due to my own positionality as a poet and educator), which is itself an inquiry-based strategy centered in portraiture. I identify as a portraitist because I believe that "the human experience has meaning in particular social, cultural, and historical contexts" (Lawrence-Lightfoot & Davis, 1997, p. 43). This is intended to help us change how we see and come to connect with the data we so often read about in professional development. Embarking upon emergent strategies requires us to "intentionally change in ways that grow our capacity to embody the just and liberated worlds we long for" (Brown, 2017, p. 3), and encountering these educators through multiple dimensions of understanding will help us in that quest.

The goal of speaking with folx who identify as social justice educators is to reveal the nuances of their work while also recognizing and honoring how they show up in the world with regard to race, class, gender, and ability. Their lived experiences are not meant to serve as a blueprint but are there to provide information that you can use to build your own social justice education toolkit in order to serve your students, your teachers, your school districts, and your respective communities. Some of these folks I knew personally and a couple I had never met before. As suggested above, this small sample size is not meant to answer large research questions connected to generalizability or popular trends. Listening to the voices of a few people with approximately 50 years of experience in education combined offers only a slice of the information out there.

It is important to note that my research process in developing these vignettes involved asking three simple questions (listed on the following page) to encourage a specific focus on social justice education practices, which of course, is part of my own biases. My biases, your biases, and our biases live and breathe within our bodies, minds, and souls. Having a clear understanding of our biases and where they come from can allow us to transform them one day at a time. Because I do not know a world that thrives on social justice education (but a world that is still afraid of it) I honor it in everything that I do to reimagine my local, historical, and global educational contexts. So, I wear that bias openly with the understanding that one day, social justice practices and education will go hand-in-hand without the resistance we see today, as evidenced by the current backlash over Critical Race Theory (CRT) in school districts across the nation.

Embracing both CRT and the methodology of portraiture (where I am both researcher and creative observer), I focus on a small group of teacher voices as a way to more intimately study the *phenomenology* of their lives and their practices. Phenomenology in this sense is the study of human experiences as illuminated through the use of a first-person perspective. You will read their words directly, and the goal is for you to be in direct conversation with each educator, as though you were attending an intimate event where everyone observes and listens with the common purpose of transforming educational systems from the inside out. Each educator offers their own lived experiences in a written testimony, and I respond using a social justice education and CRT lens, sometimes with poetic verse and sometimes as a visual artist might, painting an image for you, the reader. Part of my approach to this work also involves centering one of the core principles of emergent strategy that states, "small is good, small is all (The large is a reflection of the small)" (Brown, 2017,

p. 41). Small and intimate snapshots help us have a deeper understanding of larger themes, embracing and practicing social justice education in your work and just as importantly, in your own lives outside of work.

Let us step into the conversation now, where we center healing and justice for all students, especially students who have been historically underserved in schools for decades.

The questions I asked the educators who took part in this study were as follows:

---

1. **How do you define social justice education?**
2. **Are you a social justice educator? Why or why not?**
3. **Identify a social justice pedagogical practice you use in the classroom.**

The format of this next section includes centering the voices of the participants while responding, according to my biased interpretations, based on my lived experiences as a Black woman educator and thinker. My words will be in *italics* or **bold**, while the words of the educators will be in standard roman font. Combining our experiences in this way will elevate social justice and radical ways of being and becoming simultaneously. Each participant section will end with a Radical Love Reflection (RLR), which is a direct response from me to them, rooted in compassion, intellectual curiosity, and opportunities for growth within my Social Justice Education framework.

WHO IS JUSTIN LORDE?

I know Justin from our college days in New England. He was two years older than me and an English major. Because there were not many Black English majors at our small, liberal arts school, he became a silent guide for me, which I am sure he never knew until now, if he is reading this. The Black community at our school was tiny, so we all knew one another, even if we were not the best of friends. There was an unspoken solidarity with various levels of commitment that depended upon one's level of comfort identifying with any label for unified Blackness. And I say that confidently, considering all the ways that anti-Blackness permeates every aspect of society, as seen through the high, nationwide levels of police brutality (Levin, 2023) and the legacy of a former president who was allowed to promote his racist views on television and social media (Lopez, 2020).

I have always felt proud of Justin, particularly because at the time, many Black men did not major in English. For me, it was new and refreshing to sit alongside another Black English major at a Predominantly White Institution (PWI) in the early 2000s. I reached out to Justin on social media, where we follow one another, to ask if he would be interested in talking with me for my book and he agreed almost immediately. Justin has been an educator at a private school in New Jersey for many years. I thought his story was important to capture considering his experiences as a Black male educator who went to private school and who has worked in one for almost 20 years. Read his words, feel his story...

JUSTIN'S SOCIAL JUSTICE EDUCATION TESTIMONY

Social Justice education is education in its purest form. It's education without the politics that gets in the way of progress; it's education rooted in the individual needs of children, not the power of counties and high-profile parents; it's education that impacts the whole being and changes behavior. Social justice education is making sure that each and every child is seen, heard, affirmed, respected and valued. Social justice education is the opposite of what most schools provide today. Social justice education is revolutionary.

Social justice education is making sure that each and every child is seen, heard, affirmed, respected and valued. Social justice education is the opposite of what most schools provide today. Social justice education is revolutionary.

I like to believe that on my best days I'm a social justice educator. My first act in being a social justice educator is by being a dark-skinned Brother in this field, standing over six feet with a beard and visible tattoos. *I love the way Justin* positions his Blackness, dark skin, and height in his identification *with being a social justice educator. This truth-telling is grounded in radical acceptance and radical self-love.* My first act in being a social justice educator is being unapologetically Black in a PWI. For many of my students, I'm their first Black teacher, sadly. *Many Black students go years without having a single Black teacher, especially at PWIs.* Bringing my experiences into the classroom is a disruption; I do my best to speak my truth and provide safe spaces to discuss what other teachers shy away from. Beyond that, my days are spent paying close attention to how my students choose to identify. *Analyzing how students identify themselves is centered in their radical self-care and the multiple ways they experience their education. This is a teacher who cares deeply about his students.* Doing so allows me more insight to amplify the voices of the historically marginalized. Additionally, I try to role model how I deal with my own privilege, in hopes that it will motivate them to aspire to be better each day as well. *Black people have privilege, too! Justin names his privilege to remind us that we typically associate privilege with whiteness, however, privilege through access and education is one that I can also identify with.*

Leaning into discomfort is a social justice practice that I use in the classroom. In many ways, we've all been socialized to avoid things that make us uncomfortable. I actively promote leaning into this struggle as a necessary means of learning. Providing space for difficult conversations normalizes dialogue around things labeled taboo. As students become comfortable doing so, we can begin to be honest about some of the systems in place to prevent deep learning and access.

RADICAL LOVE REFLECTION (RLR) FOR JUSTIN LORDE

Dear Justin,

Thank you for showing up as your authentic self in these responses. I can tell that you understand the privilege you hold as a Black male educator in a Predominantly White Institution. Through your words, I am humbled by the level of vulnerability and strength you carry with you each day in your role as both educator and administrator. I wondered more about what you meant when you said "education without politics." Can education exist without politics? I would argue that education is and always will be political. However, that is my own bias and not yours. But I do believe there are ample opportunities to create more educational policies centered in social justice as a way to level the playing field for all students, especially those who are the most underserved in our society.

*I love that you name "leaning into discomfort" as a social justice education practice. I have learned in my own work that many are afraid to be uncomfortable, especially those who benefit from oppressive systems that do more harm than good. How can we impact those with the **most** privileges in the **most** systems (white cisgendered, heterosexual men) to share their access and power, to leverage educational opportunities for those who have the least access? I also wonder how well you work with your predominantly white colleagues. Do you feel free to show up as your authentic self at a PWI? Are there opportunities for you to support efforts to diversify the faculty and students? These are some of the questions that came to mind as I read your words. Obviously, these questions are not meant to be answered, but rather shared in the ways of radical honesty and love. I hope that you continue to teach and lead in the ways that feel most authentic to you while continuing to elevate the importance of SJE practices.*

Let's continue the conversation, where we listen to one another's stories as carefully as we binge our favorite Netflix series; where we read with intentionality the words of educators who align themselves with social justice and individual transformation, which is both popular and unpopular because it makes people uncomfortable.

WHO IS NADIA SUTAR?

Nadia came to our elite liberal arts college when I was a senior and she was a freshman. When I first met Nadia, she was the epitome of "preppy," with J. Crew outfits to match. Preppy refers to those who attend upper-class preparatory schools or Ivy League institutions where the dress codes often include sweater vests, blazers and khakis. More importantly, preppy clothing usually signifies a presumed level of sophistication and wealth. I never imagined we would be friends, because of my own biases at the time: that

preppy clothes equated a preppy (read white) personality. How-
ever, I was very wrong about Nadia, who was always jamming to
Bob Marley in her room or car and was a budding poet who
elevated social justice ways of knowing and being whenever we
connected. I learned to push my limited biases to the side and
embrace all that we had in common: we were two literature-loving
women of color on a college campus that was very white and very
status quo. After college, we both found ourselves teaching in
English classrooms. Nadia began her career in private schools as
an English teacher and would often share stories of the diverse
books she was teaching to highly privileged students, especially
with regard to socioeconomic background. When we traded
teaching stories, mine based in public school classrooms in
Brooklyn, NY, and hers based in many classrooms from California
to New York City, we realized we had the same mission: to change
the world through social justice teaching and learning practices.
Nadia's story is close to my heart because I consider her to be a
friend and a fellow social justice warrior.

NADIA'S SOCIAL JUSTICE EDUCATION TESTIMONY

When I think about radical love and social justice education, I first think about radical love for one's self. I struggled deeply and in complex ways to develop self-love—partly because it's human—I think—to be self critical and to internalize and project the criticisms of others. Being a racial and ethnic "other" who grew up in a predominantly white and Christian space exacerbated this perhaps innate tendency. I saw the world and myself through the lens of the white gaze (Morrison). In order to develop self-love, I had to first recognize and reject this gaze and then fall in love with my own identity—my Indian-ness and my female-ness—by unapologetically telling my story.

I love the way Nadia immediately centers herself in her narrative as Indian and female, and how she names her internalization of the white gaze while also referencing Toni Morrison (a writer we both love and discuss often in our personal conversations). Our friendship language is education, literature, and love, which is reflected in how we communicate with one another.

Through this process of identity discovery, I met and married a white man. There were so many ways in which he too was not the white Christian upper-class version of "the white male" American dream. His Irish Catholic single mother had rejected many aspects of The Dream (Coates), and he possessed a kind of otherness that was attracted to mine.

Nadia's discussion of "The Dream" is referencing journalist and author Ta-Nehisi Coates' seminal book, Between the World and Me, *where he discusses in-depth, conceptions of The American Dream, which is fictional, aspirational, and resides within the heart of racism and capitalism. We both love the book, almost as much as we love Toni Morrison. Social justice and The Dream go hand-in-hand in the sense that if we truly had an equitable playing field for all, across race, class, gender, ability, and sexuality, then everyone would have a fair chance to attain The Dream. Is The Dream really alive when only a few have access to opportunities and wealth? And when those few usually do not look like Nadia or me?*

I think that the process of creating—which means ultimately allowing yourself to find—this deep connection to your identity and a knowledge of how you are positioned in the world is at the core of social justice education and at the core of my practice as a literature teacher and social justice educator. Paulo Freire said, "The teacher is of course an artist, but being an artist does not mean that he or she can make the profile, can shape the students. What the educator does in teaching is to make it possible for the student to become themselves" (Paulo Friere, *We Make the Road by Walking, Conversations on Education and Social Change*).

I referenced Paulo Freire's Pedagogy of the Oppressed *earlier, which Nadia did not know. Our hearts are often in sync that way when it comes to social justice education. We rhyme through our words and we share what we have heard in poetic conversations rooted in radical self-care. As friends, we have sat in discomfort many times, examining what it means to be a poet, a writer, and an educator. And more importantly, what it means to be all three, with multiple identities constantly hanging on to your face, to your body, and to your spirit. Nadia brings up Freire because she sees herself as both teacher and artist while understanding that the work is never easy*

*and always pushes us to become better versions of ourselves... or
at least it should.*

What was surprising to me was how this story of self methodology (*a research process in which teachers examine their
practices through inquiry and self-reflection*) applied to white
students in pursuit of liberation and in conversations about
social identities and hierarchies. White students often struggle
traumatically with self-love when it comes to their whiteness,
their racial identity, and contending with their position in the
hierarchy. Teaching with radical love means recognizing that
even the "white," so-called Christian, upper-class and supposedly heterosexual and heteronormative male can be
suffering due to these social identifiers. Convincing those who
are reaping the benefits of and enjoying their white male
privilege of the worthiness of this kind of identity work can be
one of the most difficult tests of radical love.

*My friends are brilliant, really. And I think that is why I am even
more committed to this work, too. Because I know that I do not do
this alone, but rather in solidarity with the sistas and brothas who
do this work with me. I intentionally elevate BIPOC voices because
our narratives are either silenced or whitewashed and my "crew
can't go for that." As prophesized in the rap song "My Crew Can't
Go for That" (1996) by Trigga tha Gambler, my crew does not go for
just anything; we are really about that social justice life. An SJE life
requires us to challenge our assumptions daily, recognize our biases, and help to leave the world better than how we received it. It's
an arduous yet transformative task. And it takes radical love to
teach white upper-class students about social justice and identity
politics, especially as a Brown woman in a PWI. And Nadia did this
beautifully, through radical love and pedagogical frameworks
rooted in compassion and empathy, both critical components of
social justice education.*

However, it seems as though oppressive ideologies like white
supremacy, toxic masculinity, and heteronormativity are
destructive to all people including cis, straight white males—they
require a kind of insidious destruction of oneself to perpetuate.

*And this is a major aspect of transforming education, creating
liberation for all of us, not only some of us. Oppression harms the*

oppressor and the oppressed as Audre Lorde reminded us when she said, "the master's tools will never dismantle the master's house." Our intersectional ways of knowing, being, and becoming must align with our ability to be who we are fully, each of us, in our respective ways.

The deepest and most honest thinkers about social justice and human liberation understand the pain that oppression wreaked on the oppressor, too. What, therefore, does it mean to examine the white slave master's psyche as traumatized and how would such inquiry affect our approach to racial justice? Is it a form of radical love to feel compassion for not only our "self" but also whomever our "other" may be? White students, too, need to heal their own traumas of white supremacy in order to fully recognize the humanity of Black, Indigenous, and people of color (BIPOC) communities.

I have been constantly thinking about what freedom means as a Black woman in this body and in this world. It always feels like a dream or a reimagined reality. We cannot change history, but we can continue to push for dismantling oppressive practices every-where, especially in classrooms and schools. Radical love requires love for ourselves and our collective humanity across race, class, gender, ability, and sexuality.

There is an assumption here that white students do not see the humanity of BIPOC communities. Several events throughout cur-rent history, particularly white police officers shooting down Black children or Dylan Roof walking into a Black church and killing praying parishioners speak to this truth. We can also make space for white students who are aligned with social justice ideals due to their own upbringing, with parents who lifted up the importance of diversity, equity, and inclusion. Healing the traumas of white supremacy certainly starts at home.

In fact, I think we are realizing that the liberation of BIPOC communities cannot be achieved until these traumas of white supremacy upon the oppressor himself are addressed, cauterized, and healed. The liberation must be collective.

Only storytelling—art in its original form—can lead us to these fundamental truths, which are at the core of social justice work and radical love. All students, no matter their background, their privilege, or lack thereof need to engage in this practice of authentic storytelling in order to interrogate and contextualize their "I" and prepare themselves to feel compassion for an "other." Not all students will willingly participate. For those who do, each one of them has to feel that their story will be affirmed and be genuinely heard. This kind of restorative human work is the precursor to working together to bring about true, interconnected, and enduring justice for all.

Storytelling is definitely an aspect of the work for radical healing. It is not the only way to move closer to radical love, as Nadia states, but sharing our stories definitely creates opportunities for collective healing and critical understanding. One of the tenets of CRT is counter-storytelling, which centers the stories of those at the margins to intentionally counter dominant narratives. Dominant narratives refer to those that are the most influential throughout society and institutions. Underrepresented stories, those reflective of BIPOC, are typically not centered in mainstream culture (Castelli, 2023). Therefore, CRT counterstories echo the storytelling and social justice work that Nadia describes. Sharing stories of those at the margins with students who represent the dominant culture, while encouraging them to create their own stories, creates a space to develop radical trust and reflective healing.

Of course, the way in which we create space for this kind of storytelling is paramount. White students have to commit to being vulnerable, to admitting the shortcomings of their knowledge and perspective. It must also be recognized that many BIPOC will have experienced the same shortcomings of knowledge and perspective in some aspects of liberation work. The complexities and intersectionalities are abundant. All participants must own their mistakes, to bear witness to the pain that white supremacy has wreaked on BIPOC, pain that white individuals have been complicit in, and at times have actively inflicted. BIPOC must be willing to continue to offer emotional labor, and white people need to offer payment for this labor by transferring power in the dynamic. *Black people do not have to offer emotional labor, but if/when they do, white people should acknowledge that it is a gift and should not be an expectation. There is deep trauma associated with racial dialogues. It is noted that, "Race dialogues are ostensibly organized to help improve the conditions for racial and ethnic minorities, but they may be harming the very groups they aim to help" (Tiayon, 2020). When BIPOC engage in dialogues about race and racism when they are not ready or do not wish to participate, it can easily result in reliving traumatic experiences which can cause emotional stress. There must be relational trust among all parties and the understanding that white people have a responsibility to do their own internal work when it comes to social justice, healing, and unlearning.* What this looks like is a willingness to slow down and listen. White people therefore need to show BIPOC that trust is warranted through radical love and commitment.

This kind of transformative storytelling and social justice work, grounded in radical love for the self and the other, needs to be at the center and not the margins of educational practices. Social justice education is of secondary importance to America's education mission, and it is often carried out by those who are considered secondary to the white, heterosexual, cisgendered norm. I am reminded of writer Julia Alvarez's interpretation of the Native American trope that "the truth is in the center and you are never there, you are at different points around the circle…and the truth is all of these stories put together; all of these stories put together get at the complexity and the multiplicity of the truth instead of flattening it out to the truth, which is what is dangerous. Once you have the truth, you have the official story. You have only one possibility." What she is referring to here is a decentering of any master narrative and the idea that a multiplicity of narratives rotates around the notion of truth, which is complex, and constructed by all the voices and perspectives around it.

With our students, we must deconstruct the master narratives and assemble new and truly democratic ways of knowing and being.

RADICAL LOVE REFLECTION (RLR) FOR NADIA SUTAR

Dear Nadia,

Your commitment to social justice ways of knowing and being are clear and you do not hold back your frustrations about the perils of white supremacy. The truth-telling you exhibit through your words is rooted in the complexity of radical love. How can we offer emotional labor to someone who is oppressive, for example? Should BIPOC be expected to offer up that emotional labor when we are also literally trying to survive every day? I do not have the answers, as I too have done this as teacher, professor, and higher-education leader, so I understand your point and would argue that most BIPOC offer up emotional labor to oppressors with the hope that it will lead to our collective liberation. However, what is the role of the oppressor in their unlearning? How can we put the onus on those in positions of power? How can we get those who benefit from white privilege to take accountability and lead some of this work, too? My hope is that the social justice practices in this book will support us in that mission.

I love the way you lift up social justice warriors like Julia Alvarez and Ta-Nehisi Coates to illustrate that many scholars and thinkers were (and continue to be) committed to this work long before we printed the words on this page. This exchange between us helps to continue the ongoing conversation regarding our collective liberation through learning, loving, and radical healing. I also hope, though, that those in positions of power who have access to more resources and privilege, will leverage their power by leaning into liberatory practices like storytelling, not because they were forced to, but rather because they understand that our collective humanity depends upon it, as does the possibility of a more socially just world.

WHO IS FREDERICK MENSAH?

I met Frederick in graduate school while completing my doctoral work in New York City. Frederick, also pursuing his doctorate at the time, stood out as a Black male science educator, a reality you do not witness often (African Americans comprise just 9% of the American STEM workforce, and the U.S. Department of Education estimates that just 2% of teachers are Black men). We are both committed to social justice aligned work, through hip-hop education specifically. Hip-hop and graduate school, the two points where we intersect, helped us develop a friendship centered in relational trust and mutual respect. The way he merges science and hip-hop education through creativity and scholarship is incredible. I have always admired his commitment to developing a love of science among mostly Black and Brown students in urban communities. It reminded me of a lot of the work I did in my English classroom back in the day, using hip-hop to illustrate creative storytelling through culturally relevant teaching and learning practices. As a result, Frederick and I connected through our personal lived experiences as teachers turned graduate students, where we studied vast theories to elevate hip-hop education practices.

After completing graduate school, Frederick became a professor in New Jersey, where I was also a professor and director of education at another university at the time. I remember him reaching out to connect on issues in teacher education from a social justice lens. And that is how Frederick often situates himself, always as a learner and a leader, committed to radical collaboration and collective teaching and learning practices.

FREDERICK'S SOCIAL JUSTICE TESTIMONY

Social justice education refers to teaching and learning that encourages participants to make sense of and be critical of systems, structures, and policies that oppress any group of people. To me, social justice education teaches the histories and narratives of historically marginalized groups, as well as how these groups have been repeatedly marginalized. Finally, social justice education empowers participants to create social change in their local and global communities.

Immediately, Frederick reminds us that to embody social justice education, you have to carefully examine systems that are oppressive. Similarly, he notes that centering the stories of those at the margins is how we begin to leverage positional and historical power to transform communities from the inside out, which reminds me of Nadia's push for storytelling as a transformative pedagogical practice.

I identify as a social justice educator because, in each class that I teach, I teach the history of historically underrepresented groups (through science and hip-hop education), the challenges that they face, and what students can do to support underrepresented populations. Finally, I teach students how to build ties with the community to support student learning.

Frederick connects his work as a social justice educator directly to the communities that we serve, centering both theory and practice. Too often, in educational books and research, we either over-emphasize theory without a direct connection to pedagogy or we are overly practical, neglecting the theories that inform and improve teaching and learning.

A social justice practice I use in the classroom includes analyzing data from various school districts in NJ and comparing districts by race and class to highlight and draw conclusions about disparities in educational access across the state.

Analyzing differences across school districts amplifies a CRT focus, which includes looking at how funding for school districts is directly dependent upon access to resources based on community. As we explored in Chapter 3, historically low-income and predominantly Black communities (which also tend to have lower property taxes) directly impact the quality of education in the surrounding community. A wondering I have is, after having students look at data across school districts that focus on educational disparities, how are these students taught to become better teachers? In what ways will they leverage having this information? Helping students in teacher education programs learn how to turn data into transformative teaching and learning practices is crucial when it comes to implementing social justice practices in the classroom and in the community.

RADICAL LOVE REFLECTION (RLR) FOR FREDERICK MENSAH

Dear Frederick,

We have both come a long way since graduate school and I am glad that we are still connected. I can see your intentional focus on educational disparity data and a desire to effect enduring change in schools. As a professor of educational studies, I know that your students, colleagues, and university are lucky to have you on their side. I also know, through having an understanding of your journey, that you have been committed to this work for over a decade. I hope that as you continue to elevate in your professional journey as a professor, you continue to have more opportunities to make social justice education an intentional and iterative practice in higher-education classrooms and in the various science education communities that you are a part of. Because science is often thought of as more factual than creative (which is not true), I am glad to know that your work blends science with hip-hop to spark creativity, while giving young people a deeper connection to science as a holistic subject that can be culturally relevant and social justice-aligned, if led by people who are as committed as you are. Some examples of how to merge science with hip-hop in holistic ways include:

- *Allowing students to create scientific raps, combining their daily experiences with scientific theories they learn*

- *Giving students multiple opportunities to explore the history of hip-hop and its relation to their physical environments, which is directly connected to science*

- *Having students move around the classroom often, to tap into the kinesthetic aspects of learning. Movement, such as breakdancing, is also one of the five elements of hip-hop*

I stand in solidarity with you, always, as we continue to share mutual colleagues while creating intentional opportunities for critical hope and radical love.

INTERMISSION

The conversation will shift now, as I will introduce you to two educators who I do not know personally. I came to know these educators on X, when I put out a call for individuals who identify as social justice educators to reach out to me. Although several educators were interested, the testimonies of the educators you are about to meet stood out the most. I am mindful that the intimacy of my language will shift, since I do not have a personal relationship with these educators. However, their testimonies are important for painting a full picture of the nuances in social justice education teaching and learning practices.

WHO IS RICHARD TATE?

Richard Tate is a white male educator and counselor who reached out to me on X after I posted a tweet calling for anyone who identifies as a social justice educator and who would be willing to share their lived experiences with me for an upcoming book. Richard seemed excited to be a part of this work. Communicating with him on social media, and eventually via email, was pleasant and informative. Richard entered the education field through counseling, which I find fascinating, particularly because counseling is a practice inherently connected to radical self-care and healing. Those who are concerned with what is happening in the hearts and minds of students are doing social justice work in many ways. We cannot truly help students if we are not concerned with the emotional and spiritual conditions of their being.

RICHARD TATE'S TESTIMONY

Social justice education is the promotion of critical consciousness as a means to liberate the individual from societal oppression, while combating the further institutionalization of this oppression and its impact on others, particularly those who have access to the fewest personal, familial, group, and societal resources.

Richard's definition of social justice education echoes the importance of societal oppression and institutionalized racism mentioned in Nadia and Fredericks' testimonies. Dismantling oppression is a key component of SJE. A question that immediately comes to mind is how someone from a privileged background like Richard's can combat oppression. What consistent, daily actions can white people take to support social justice? Especially white cisgendered men, who benefit from capitalism, systems of oppression, and the institution of racism? They can begin by acknowledging one's positional power and making daily efforts to push against inequity.

This question (about being a social justice educator) assumes an absolute, of which I cannot claim to belong to at all times. I am actively working toward having a social justice practice, but this activity is a daily effort that requires ongoing attention and energy. As a white male, I was born with immense privilege, and society (which is built upon white male privilege) easily reinforces this fact every day. Thus, awareness of my own privilege is something that I am constantly reminding myself of.

But awareness of one's privilege as a white male is not enough. The awareness must be coupled with daily and intentional actions that leverage one's positional power as a pathway for creating more equity for those who are consistently "othered," such as BIPOC.

But my work in education is not just about my own self-awareness. It is also about raising the consciousness of the young people that I am working with.

An SJE framework reminds us that this awareness is a collective experience, not only from teacher to student but from student to teacher, as well. We help build students" awareness and they help build our awareness. Thus, in my classroom and counseling practice, I actively seek to engage young people in the grappling of ideas. For example: What does class mean? What choices do I have that are afforded to me because of my class? These are common questions you may encounter in my history curriculum. But, the mere grappling with these ideas is not enough. I also engage young people in questions around action. "What can I do as a result of my understanding?" and "How can I make different choices with the knowledge I now have?" are questions that I will often ask students. These questions are designed to raise critical consciousness and promote a social justice orientation among my students. Furthermore, they are designed to raise awareness of the experiences of others, to encourage reflection on one's place in the world, and to foster empathy and understanding of the existence of systemic oppression.

I love the centering of empathy through critical consciousness and self-reflection. I am reminded of the heart chakras I touched on in the introduction. Social justice work is heart work, always and forever. If we can truly see one another, we can radically love one another to effect systemic changes within education and in our respective communities.

A significant dichotomous challenge any K-12 educator faces is that young people in this age bracket are often under the care of their parents. On one hand, parents are a teacher's single most important resource and one of their biggest advocates. On the other hand, parents' control much of the young person's life, often allowing for limited personal agency.

I worry about Robert's perception of the role of parents in this work. His language seems to "other" parents as part of this process and labels them under the guise of "control." An SJE framework requires parent participation, as well. As social justice educators, parents' ways of knowing and being must be acknowledged in order to fully support the students we have the privilege of working with.

A pedagogical practice I often engage young people in is the encouragement of and training around courageous conversations. *It is important to cite the Black male educator and strategist Glenn Singleton here, who is the creator of courageous conversations, a protocol designed to have difficult conversations about race.* This is often Socratic in nature in my classroom or in my office, but I am constantly pushing to have students engage in these courageous conversations outside of the classroom as well. For example, in ninth-grade history class, we study the dietary habits of Early Humans, and how our bodies have developed over millennia. This is coupled with a project through which students are encouraged to engage their parents in a series of conversations about their household eating habits and food purchasing habits. *In order for this activity to be social justice aligned, we must take into account that food insecurity is a real struggle for many families and household eating habits and food purchases are often a direct reflection of that.* Needless to say, these conversations have a range of results, but the practice is what is fundamentally important. Having young people articulate their beliefs and stand up for something to a close family member is terrific training for future conversations around the dinner table (or holidays!) in which they will inevitably have to engage in far more controversial topic discussions. Clarity of argument and willingness to speak to power are critical social justice practices.

Encouraging students to engage in courageous conversations is a powerful practice. However, there seems to be a theme in Richard's words of having students critique their families and parents. If Richard's students are BIPOC students, these activities must be more structured to acknowledge the distinction among students' diverse lived experiences and their parents' cultural ways of knowing, being and belonging. I would also encourage Richard to invite parents into his classroom as thought partners and even to engage in some of the in-class courageous conversations as a way to bridge the school and home divide that often occurs throughout the schooling process.

RADICAL LOVE REFLECTION (RLR) FOR RICHARD TATE

Dear Richard,

Thank you for being open and vulnerable to my questions about being a social justice educator. I also appreciate your willingness to be a part of this project although we do not know one another personally. I noticed you lifted up the privileges that you have as a white man who is interested in using social justice as a tool to elevate students' overall lives through counseling and transformative teaching and learning practices. As you continue to do this healing work, this heart work, I think it would be helpful to learn more about the parents of the students you serve. Too often, parents are left out of social justice pedagogy and including them can strengthen the divide that often happens between home and school, especially for students who are at the margins and live in historically underserved communities.

As you continue to do this work as both counselor and educator, I hope that radical love and the diversity of the communities you serve continue to inform your practices, not only for your students, but also for yourself, your family, and the communities that you are a part of. I know you said that you believe that claiming to be a social justice educator is "an absolute" of sorts. I encourage you to reconsider it as the right thing to do, rather than an "absolute," especially with your positionality as a white male with access to privilege and power.

WHO IS ELENA DE JESUS?

Elena De Jesus is a passionate educator who was very excited to be a part of this project. Immediately, I could see Elena's passion through the words in her email and her rapid responses to my questions for this chapter. It was such a pleasure communicating with her, and her commitment to being a key voice in this timely work certainly warmed me up to her. I understand that Elena has an extensive background practicing social justice teaching and learning practices as a teacher, as an administrator AND as a leader who has a background in Special Education. Elena also identifies as a Black woman and offers another diverse perspective in this ongoing conversation regarding social justice education.

ELENA DE JESUS' SOCIAL JUSTICE TESTIMONY

Social justice education includes providing equitable opportunities to all students and advocating for all students, especially students in vulnerable populations (i.e., Black students, students with disabilities, students who live and attend schools in areas that are considered to be at a socioeconomic disadvantage, etc.)

Elena's definition of SJE centers all students, especially those who are typically at the margins. She is the only educator who I spoke to that centered students with disabilities, who are often erased when discussing equitable outcomes. But how can we discuss social justice without discussing Special Education (which is exactly why my previous chapter is so important)?

I'd like to consider myself a social justice educator and administrator who practices, embodies and encourages others to be social justice educators. I've been an educator for about 10 years and I have worked in cities such as Trenton, Paterson, and Newark, New Jersey; Baltimore, Maryland; and Washington D.C. What I've seen within these cities and schools is that Black students lack opportunity, leading to an opportunity gap. And students with disabilities are often mistreated, or their parents are misled because they are not aware of their rights as a parent of a student with a disability. In my role as a social justice educator, I've never been too afraid or timid to advocate for these students. It often puts me on the wrong side of administrators for calling them out and stating facts, and [referring to] laws for how they are not meeting the needs of students or providing a free APPROPRIATE public education.

The opportunity gap that Elena discusses, along with calling out the legality of the treatment of students with disabilities amplifies, a CRT understanding of the ways that laws uphold educational inequities. To shift policies that directly impact the most vulnerable student populations, we must call out inequities when we see them. Too many educators are willing to remain silent, keeping oppressive teaching, learning, and leadership practices intact, while continuing to cause harm to students, especially Black students and students with disabilities.

One example of a social justice pedagogy practice that I have used in my class is giving students the opportunity to share their experiences through free verse poetry. Students have spoken about their experiences in other classrooms and programs and how the "n" word being used by white teachers makes them feel. *There is never an excuse for a white teacher to use the "n" word. You will immediately lose the trust of your Black students.* Another student spoke about his experience as a young Black male tempted by his surroundings, and who compares himself to Mike Brown from Ferguson [Missouri], wondering if he's next. *Many Black students live in a space of perpetual trauma based on the ongoing violence against Black bodies by police, as discussed in my introduction.* I allowed my students to see how poetry has provided myself (a Black educator) an opportunity to heal by sharing my own feelings and experiences through my own poetry. My students have also had the opportunity to perform the powerful pieces at A Taste of Newark, an annual black tie event held at the renowned New Jersey Performing Arts Center (NJPAC), also known as the New Jersey Center for Performing Arts is located in Downtown Newark and is one of the largest performing arts centers in the United States.

As a poet, I am particularly in love with this aspect of Elena's work. As an English educator, I often used poetry to help students discuss difficult issues. In fact, poetry was often the pathway to have the courageous conversations Richard touched upon. Being vulnerable with her students through her own poetry helps to bridge the power divide between student and teacher, a common issue in classrooms all around the world. When we see students as equal contributors to the teaching and learning process and not as subordinates, we can achieve a more socially just learning environment. Giving students the opportunity to perform at the New Jersey Performing Arts Center (NJPAC) is a powerful way of lifting up students' voices and choices in prominent spaces.

I've gone to bat for my special education students. One particular young man had been in the school system for five to six years but his disability was misunderstood. He was constantly mistreated by staff and by his own mother. *This is the case for many BIPOC students with disabilities, unfortunately. I* witnessed this too many times among Black students with special needs, as discussed in the previous chapter. Mid-school year, he was placed in foster care and went through about five different foster homes, and several state-appointed social workers. He ultimately ended up in an all-boys foster facility because his mother didn't want him and she ended up in prison.

Due to his disability, he was impulsive and would steal. A white administrator thought that a restorative practice assignment, of having the student do a presentation on how stealing pushes students into the school-to-prison pipeline, would help. In this case, as an educator and as an administrator, I had to advocate for my student, especially when the school-to-prison pipeline is more about the no-tolerance policies within schools than the fact that he took something that didn't belong to him. *I am grateful that Elena was in a position to support and protect this young Black boy as he struggled at home and in school to be heard.* I told her he would not be writing nor presenting that assignment to the two white women he stole from. Ultimately, this issue was taken to the director of Special Education and she put an end to it because this wasn't something that needed to end up in the press. This is one incident of me fighting for my students and there is so much more to his story and so many other students.

I feel the deep pain in Elena's words as a social justice educator fighting against racism to protect her students. Going up against racism always feels like trying to sprint in the sand, seemingly going fast at times, while remaining stuck in place at other times. A commitment to social justice requires us to call out racism, homophobia, sexism, ageism and every other ideology that maintains the oppression of a marginalized group of people. Protecting a student who is being oppressed right before your eyes will require a commitment to sitting in discomfort, and it can sometimes come at the cost of your job …

RADICAL LOVE REFLECTION (RLR) FOR ELENA DE JESUS

Dear Elena,

Thank you for showing up as a radical Critical Race Theorist who stood up to oppressive administrators in order to protect your students. I could feel your journey through your testimony, which demonstrated radical self-care for yourself and for your students. They are so lucky to have had you as a teacher and to have you now as an educational leader and administrator. I, too, have stood up to instances of racism throughout my career, as a teacher, teacher-educator, professor, and higher-education leader. What I have often come to realize is that few people actually call out racism when they see it in schools. It is almost as if everyone becomes paralyzed by racism, allowing it to be a perpetual monster, ruining many lives in the process. Thank you for standing up and standing out when it was hard to do so. However, that is what radical love and an SJE framework supported by CRT can do for educational systems: shed light on the wrongs and create more equity for all students.

Thank you, Black woman, for continuing to elevate your radical consciousness by leading with love and liberation in spaces that are often quick to silence such bold actions. I see you and I stand in solidarity with you, always.

POST CONVERSATION TAKEAWAYS

I hope you enjoyed reading the testimonies of this diverse and thoughtful group of educators, each with drastically different educational and lived experiences. As you read their words, I hope you could envision your own practices alongside them. Not necessarily to compare, but rather to help create a collective vision of social justice education practices in theory and in action. Transforming educational systems from the inside out cannot be done in isolation but must be endeavored as a collective movement facilitated by love and elevated by a radical consciousness through social justice.

I found myself deeply humbled by their words, as it is always a gift when teachers share their personal stories with me. Seeing the similarities and distinctions among their stories reminded me that educators are always at the helm of our future, helping to guide curious minds from racially, culturally, and linguistically diverse backgrounds.

I also hope this chapter decentered my voice and made room for the contributions of other narratives. I did this to model social justice teaching and learning practices that use portraiture as an approach to research, and to emphasize how

CTT can work on a broad scale. Collaborating with others is how we lead with love instead of hierarchy. When was the last time you allowed students to lead a class discussion? Have you ever engaged in reciprocal teaching, where a student teaches a concept to the class that the teacher has already taught? Reciprocal teaching practices allow teachers and students to build relational trust, which leads to higher academic outcomes for all students. We have to learn to trust our students just as much as we need to learn to trust other perspectives that may be outside of our comfort zones. Push yourself to consume literature, social media content, books, television shows, and podcasts from individuals you don't know enough about. It is easy to stay in our bubbles and only hang out with like-minded people. But when we really embrace SJE, we begin to understand that as much as we practice it professionally, we must also be willing to practice it personally in the communities that we identify with; at the dinner table with family members who model oppression; among friends who say hateful things about other groups of people. We cannot turn social justice practices off and on like a light switch. To become a social justice educator is to become a lifelong ally to fighting oppression on every single level across race, class, gender, ability, and sexuality.

As a way to honor the transformative teaching strategies shared by the educators in this chapter, here are some key SJE practices that you can implement in your classroom:

1. **Storytelling:** Create multiple opportunities for students to share their stories and honor their cultural ways of knowing and being in the classroom. This encourages students to celebrate their multifaceted identities and in turn allows them to be their authentic selves. Examples of storytelling activities include: writing first-person narratives, developing song lyrics, and creating first-person videos and community-related videos. Students are at the center of our curriculum. Anything we teach should have our students' voices and experiences at the center, which increases engagement and equitable student outcomes.

2. **Courageous Conversations:** Engaging in courageous conversations to address difficult topics such as racism, violence, poverty, and injustice helps to deepen trust and

understanding among students, teachers, and school leaders. Students should also be provided with ample opportunities to critique the various systems they are a part of, such as educational systems, healthcare systems, community resources, etc. This encourages them to expand their understanding of how they fit into the equation and offers them a chance to formulate ways they can improve these systems. Courageous Conversations can happen across subject areas and should have a particular theme and a leader to facilitate the discussion. To disrupt the traditional hierarchy and create more equitable opportunities for leadership, that leader can be a student instead of a teacher or school administrator.

3. **Poetry:** Writing poetry is an important creative option for students in all subject areas. When students are allowed to express themselves creatively among their peers, they build more confidence in themselves. Creativity is a drastically underrated resource in classrooms, especially in the age of standardized testing and post-COVID-19, where so-called learning loss continues to dominate educational content. Allowing students to use poetry as a tool to amplify their individual perspectives also creates opportunities for counter-storytelling, a tenant of CRT, as explained earlier in the chapter. Some examples of using poetry in the classroom include having students write poems about themes relevant to a current problem in the world, in their local communities, or in their schools. Provide time for students to publicly share these poems with their peers and in the larger school community to celebrate their voices.

4. **Analyzing Community Data:** Teaching our students to be researchers, particularly in a digital age, is crucial to an SJE framework. Start by having your students examine the local statistics of their respective communities. They could look at average income, average education levels, healthcare access, and graduation rates. Having students analyze localized data can increase their connection to their communities while helping to develop a critical social justice eye. When we treat our students as researchers of their lives and communities alongside the curriculum, we are modeling SJE by having students speak back to their

daily realities, while actively bridging the divide between home and school. Some community data analysis activities include group research projects that solve a community issue, writing positional papers about issues impacting their school using school statistics as evidence, and group debates about a controversial issue in the world using global data as a resource (i.e., global literacy trends, the role of poverty and access to education, etc.).

5. **Become Comfortable with Discomfort:** In order to practice social justice pedagogy and leadership, we must become comfortable with sitting in discomfort. It is only through struggle that we can truly progress collectively, as the late great abolitionist and former slave Frederick Douglass taught us in his autobiography. As echoed through the words of the educators in this book, discomfort is always part of doing the work and that means being committed to SJE daily, not only when it benefits us or makes us look good. There is an intentional activism through SJE that honors students' lived experiences while contributing to the surrounding school community through leveraging resources and social-emotional support mechanisms. It means you have to call out poor leadership practices rooted in racism. It means that you have to know your biases in order to challenge them. It means you have to show up every single day with the understanding that lives are literally on the line and you are in a unique position to be the change you actively seek in your life and in the lives of your students and their families.

This chapter provided an opportunity for you to experience the words of educators who are of diverse teaching backgrounds and identities through portraiture, which is a creative, conversational and unique research method that honors radical storytelling.

Each educator has a common goal: to use social justice as a tool to transform students' lives.

Learning more about each educator reveals that we are all coming to this work with various starting points, however, that does not take away from the level of impact we can have upon our students every day. The work is challenging yet rewarding, and it is important to continue to make space for all students' voices within schooling systems that have historically practiced oppressive teaching and learning methods. If we are committed to students' ongoing freedom inside and outside of the classroom, supporting and developing social justice educators is an important strategy in all schools.

CHAPTER 6

Where Do We Go From Here?

As a culture worker who belongs to an oppressed people my job is to make revolution irresistible. (Toni Cade Bambara)

So where do we go from here? It is easy to talk the talk, but much harder to practice the ideas that can transform education. You have walked with me through the journey of this book, reading the radical love notes, expanding your understanding of Critical Race Theory, and learning from the insights granted by portraiture. We discussed pedagogical extension activities that can elevate social justice teaching and learning practices while learning about some of the experiences that shaped my journey as an educator and thought leader. At the beginning, I asked you to focus on the power of radical love and your heart as a reminder of our collective humanity. Let's review the key points that were highlighted in the book between then and now:

1. A Social Justice Education (SJE) model is centered on radical love and liberation. Practicing SJE requires loving students in holistic and intentional ways.

2. It is important to understand the needs of your students while leveraging your biases and positional power to provide equitable outcomes for all.

3. An SJE requires an *unlearning* process that incorporates self-reflection, radical self-care, and conscious community-building inside and outside of the classroom.

4. The Radical Love Activities provided in Chapters 1–4 are meant to shift oppressive classroom culture through pedagogical activities rooted in social justice and radical love. These activities can happen in any discipline and serve as moments for recentering and reimagining what the classroom can become once relational trust is improved among teachers, students, and school leaders.

5. A successful SJE classroom allows students the freedom to be fully authentic. They feel safe being their full selves and are not punished for expressing who they are.

6. Special Education is an extension of social justice teaching and learning practices and should include a curriculum that is engaging and humanizing for students with special needs. Identifying students with special needs requires a holistic process with trained educators who can carefully assess the needs of a student to avoid the overrepresentation of Black/Brown boys in Special Education.

7. Teachers and school leaders must intentionally develop and sustain classrooms and schools that honor liberation and the fight against white supremacy. We all have a responsibility to push against the status quo by creating classroom and school cultures that embrace equity through the curriculum and leadership.

8. The lived experiences of social justice educators are diverse and reveal nuances across race, class, and gender. No experience is the same but all social justice teaching and learning practices honor students' ways of knowing and being.

I am reminded of the words of the late scholar and writer James Baldwin in his essay, "A Talk to Teachers," (1963) where he discusses the important role teachers play in changing the world. Baldwin argues, "The paradox of education is precisely this—that as one begins to become conscious one begins to examine the society in which he is being educated." When we make social justice the center of how we teach and learn, we make space for our critical consciousness as well as the consciousness of our students. Transformative learning and radical self-care processes are only possible when students and educators are free enough to critique the society and systems they are a part of. It is imperative that we create spaces where such transformation and care are possible.

The lessons shared in this book are meant to inform a continuous cycle of improvement in schools and classrooms. A continuous cycle of improvement recognizes that there will be mistakes and iterations along the way. Mistakes are unavoidable when you aim to meet the needs of everyone who is involved in the work of *doing* SJE. As a result, being committed to these SJE practices requires short-term and long-term goals that center student growth and overall equity depending on their respective needs. Radical love and self-care are the building blocks, which are either deprioritized or completely missing from much of the work done in the education industry. We often talk about self-care as independent of education or as a special moment to disrupt classroom and school experiences. My charge, and my hope for the educators reading this book, is to make radical self-care practices an intentional aspect of teaching and learning, in a way that honors our differences, our collective stories, our struggles and traumas, and our human right to critical growth and healing.

In embracing a non-linear and radical approach to SJE, my approach is intentionally loving, supportive, and humanistic in its pursuits. I know that I am not the first nor last person to discuss social justice teaching and learning practices. However, I know that merging SJE with my radical self-care framework is unique and timely, particularly in a post-COVID world, where we have lost many of our dear friends, family members, and neighbors. Taking care of ourselves and one another is essential to developing relational trust and more humanizing educational spaces. This work is elevated through my coaching business, Self Love Life 101, where I work with individuals, institutions, and organizations to change the world through SJE and radical self-care practices.

As you consumed the words of the educators in the previous chapter, I hope it became evident that committing to being a social justice educator is no easy task. But however difficult it might be, social justice is not an *option*. If we are not concerned with social justice, we are not concerned with human rights. And if we are not concerned with human rights, our hearts have become hardened by the status quo and the ways of the world that reserve power and privilege for a select few.

As you approach the end of the book, you may be asking, "Now that I have read and embraced these ideas, does that make me a social justice educator?" I have created a helpful SJE checklist below for you to determine if you are in fact *practicing* SJE. There is a difference between being a social justice educator and doing social justice work, which are both ongoing, iterative processes. A social justice educator centers students' voices while creating culturally responsive and rigorous teaching and learning opportunities that reimagine the relationships between students and teachers. An SJE framework provides students opportunities to teach and learn, and teachers have the space to be vulnerable in order to model empathy and radical love through their leadership in the classroom. Doing social justice work goes beyond the classroom and extends to the work we do in our respective communities and personal lives. Some examples include identifying local organizations such as various chapters of the American Civil Liberties Union (ACLU) and getting involved with community initiatives. Another way to do social justice work is to donate to non-profit organizations that elevate the voices of Black, Indigenous, and people of color (BIPOC) through clear fundraising events and opportunities such as the National Urban League (https://nul.org/) and Color of Change (https://colorofchange.org/about/). As I said above, mistakes will be made in this work. It's less important *who you are now* and more important *who you want to be* for your students. What will you strive to become? Feel free to use this checklist as a way to constantly check in with yourself and your teaching/leadership practices.

SOCIAL JUSTICE EDUCATOR CHECKLIST

- ☐ I am aware of my various identities and how it shows up in the classroom/school setting.
- ☐ I self-reflect often and constantly check my biases to ensure I am providing equitable outcomes for all students.
- ☐ I understand my positionality (based on race, class, gender, and ability) and the privileges I am afforded, as a result.
- ☐ It is my job to create an inclusive classroom culture that makes all my students feel welcomed and psychologically safe.
- ☐ My curriculum is reflective of all my students across race, class, culture, gender, sexuality, and ethnicity.
- ☐ I practice radical self-care by making time to rest, recharge, and heal in order to be my best self on a daily and consistent basis.
- ☐ My students have ample opportunities to make curriculum suggestions as a way to honor their perspectives and lived experiences.
- ☐ I work with leadership to elevate student learning targets and assessments through social justice teaching and learning methods.
- ☐ I actively work with parents to cultivate healthy connections between school and home.
- ☐ Radical love is at the center of my teaching and learning practices.

 Available for download at **resources.corwin.com/RadicalLove**

PRACTICING WHAT WE PREACH

We have all been there: that moment when we say one thing and do another. We claim that we will put the needs of all students first. However, when we are pushed by leadership to "follow protocol" or to "teach to the test," we quickly put equity and social justice on the back burner. Having a checklist is one thing. Having a strategic action plan for making social justice and culturally responsive practices the norm in your classroom is another thing altogether, and it is the only way your work will move from theory to action.

When I was a high school English teacher at a school that was leading with a culture of fear instead of liberation, my daily interactions with my colleagues and administration were filled with deep anxiety. I was operating with a scripted test prep curriculum that sucked the joy out of learning. As a new teacher, for the first few months, I followed every protocol my administration enforced because I was afraid of receiving "a letter in my file," a common threat repeated by the Assistant Principal at almost every meeting. As a result, my students were miserable during every lesson, since they were filled with hundreds of multiple-choice questions and the infamous five-paragraph essays that stripped them of their critical thinking and creativity.

That was my first year of teaching and I can honestly say that, although my life outside of school was very much about activism and social justice, inside of the school, poor leadership turned me into a robot operating in a space of control and oppression. Seeing the looks on my students' faces during those tragic lessons made going to work stressful. So, what did I do during that first year? After three months of playing an educational game that did more harm than good (to my students and myself), I came up with a strategic action plan to be the social justice educator I knew that I was, based on my lived experiences as an activist and performance poet. I started creating my own lessons, which used the scripted curriculum but went far beyond them. I used the same learning objectives, but I went about it with a twist. I started incorporating culturally relevant texts such as news articles about the students' local communities, contemporary music, and song lyrics (their favorite!), and I offered spoken word end-of-unit assessments that were connected to the literary themes covered in the scripted curriculum. It was a more student-centered approach to teaching and learning. My students were happier, and more liberated in my classroom, and, more importantly, they learned that I loved them for whom they were individually. Once students realize that you love them and want the best for them, learning becomes a process of exploration and growth as opposed to fear and control.

This so-called radical approach was unpopular. When the Assistant Principal first walked into my classroom, she failed to notice my social justice-inspired teaching tactics, primarily because the learning objectives were the same as the scripted curriculum. But because my students expressed their excitement about listening to and using hip-hop to create first-person narratives, and because they were happy to have an open-mic poetry night at school, school leadership eventually figured out what I was doing. It was eventually exposed and I did receive many "letters in my file." I did not lose my job, however, because it was clear that my students were learning and thriving.

I took that risk because I could. I was young, I did not have a family at the time, and I was willing to lose it all in the name of social justice. I recognize that this is not everyone's experience and that it may come across as privileged. To a certain extent it was privileged because although I was not making a lot of money, I had the confidence in myself that if I lost my job for doing what was right for my students' basic humanity and educational success, I would find another job that was more aligned with my values as a teacher. And this is eventually what happened two years later when I left and accepted the best public-school teaching job I have ever had at Brooklyn Love School.

With that in mind, I want to ask again: What are you willing to lose to incorporate an SJE framework into your classroom? It is a task that involves serious risks, but the rewards for yourself and your students will be enduring. Why shouldn't your students feel deeply loved while being excited about learning? Why is that a radical concept? Why do many students and educators feel hopeless? Especially in the most vulnerable and overpoliced communities, where healthcare and housing inequities are rampant. Shifting harmful educational practices requires courage. You must prepare your heart for the battles that come with doing what is right. If you are unionized, ensure that you understand your rights as a teacher. That is another privilege I had during my tenure as a middle school and high school English teacher. I knew what the administration could and could not do according to my contract. I used that information to create a stronger classroom culture for my students where radical love, culturally relevant materials, safety, and trust were always at the forefront. My classroom was not perfect but it was always academically and socially elevated through a love for and a commitment to social justice. For those of you who do not have a union behind you, make sure you read the school handbook to understand your rights as a teacher. Create internal and external support systems among your colleagues because we cannot do this work in isolation. If it is not aligned with social justice ways of knowing and becoming, we must be willing to share our resources and experiences with one another to push against the larger school culture.

FINAL ACTION STEPS

Thank you for taking this journey with me, through the ups and downs of teaching, learning, loving, and reimagining how we can do better. It is all possible through a process of unlearning the harm that lives so casually within the heart of our nation's educational systems. Thank you for listening to the classroom experiences that made me question myself as a teacher almost daily. I shared these lived experiences to remind you that I have made many mistakes along the way because I am flawed and human. I am constantly learning and unlearning. What always remained the same was my commitment to giving all my students the best learning experiences possible using a culture of love and support for their respective identities and ways of knowing. I encourage you to use my successes and struggles in the classroom as inspiration for your own work.

I dare you to take the steps necessary to embrace an SJE framework. Look at the school culture that you are currently a part of. A social justice-inspired school culture honors students' identities in a holistic and humanizing way. To *do* social justice means doing it *tirelessly*: there are no days off because the lives of students and families are on the line. Step into radical love and push into the spaces where you can. In the spaces where fear is still ruling your heart, find communities that are committed to this work and learn more in order to do more for your students and, of course, for yourself, as an educator, leader, or school support staff.

Developing an SJE mindset is one thing. Sustaining it is another, as it can lead to exhaustion and burnout due to the resistance that you will face. Allowing such burnout is the opposite of a radical self-care practice. We have to take care of ourselves in the process, which means we have to rest, move our bodies, and recognize that *this is not savior work*. This is community healing work and it takes time to build momentum. Take deep breaths, meditate, and remember to have fun inside and outside of the classroom. Every day, we can push for more understanding across our differences, more collective liberation, more relational trust, and more equitable opportunities for the students we serve.

Last, but certainly not least, I want to remind you that our struggles are intimately connected. We have a responsibility to uplift our collective humanity. Each of us has unique privileges that we can effectively use to transform education from the inside out. We are all culture workers, shifting, shaping, and sealing ourselves into the memories of our students every single day. Think about what you want students to remember about being in your classroom or school community. Is your goal solely to teach them a lesson or to help them master the lessons and create their own while changing the world in the process? Continue to remind students that you *see* them for who they are while giving them the tools to critique, question, and recreate classroom spaces that are more inclusive, radically honest, and boldly loving. I dare you to be the change you seek for your students, for yourself, and for future generations that you will never meet but will leave an indelible mark upon, due to the absence of fear, while leading with love and with your heart.

NEXT STEPS FOR TEACHERS TO EMBRACE AN SJE MODEL

- Learn more about the community you work in as a way to have a more holistic understanding of where your students are coming from and the role of the school in the particular community.

- Identify your strengths as a teacher and your weaknesses. How do your strengths contribute to an SJE model? How do your weaknesses prevent you from doing this important work in your classroom? Reflect on this in a journal entry to confront your fears.

- Get students involved! Ask students often what they would like to learn on a quarterly basis (every quarter or marking period) and incorporate some of their suggestions directly into your curriculum/lesson plans. Students will feel valued as a result of this pedagogical strategy.

- Be honest with yourself through continuous journaling about your work toward becoming a social justice educator. Some prompts to include are: **(1) What are your goals for your classes and why? (2) What goals do students have for the class and why?**

- Create a community of colleagues whom you can bounce ideas off about SJE while developing and sustaining a Critical Friends Protocol (Costa & Kallick, 1993), where you observe one another's classes on a consistent basis to ensure you are being held accountable for social justice teaching, learning, and healing practices in your classroom. The overall purpose of the Critical Friends Protocol is to build a community among colleagues that is directly connected to student learning and growth, especially from a social justice lens.

NEXT STEPS FOR LEADERS TO EMBRACE AN SJE MODEL

- Decide the vision and mission of your school and update school sites and official materials to reflect a model that is grounded in SJE. For example, "Our school is committed to providing a culture of belonging and psychological safety for all students across race, gender identity, learning styles and cultural ways of knowing."

- Create ongoing professional development opportunities for teachers that discuss what SJE is and what it is not. Encourage teachers to bring student work to these professional development sessions, as a way for them to have time to analyze and reflect on student learning and development.

- Have monthly observations of teacher classrooms with an SJE rubric that incorporates differentiated learning styles for all students and centers academic rigor and student engagement.

- Provide opportunities for teachers to lead professional development sessions to showcase SJE pedagogical practices that cultivate a culture of continuous growth academically and socially in the classroom among students.

- Develop community partnerships with local organizations that provide additional teaching and learning opportunities for students and teachers through field trips, community organizing, and expanding parental engagement.

These strategies for teachers and leaders are reminders of what we can do to get started today. Sometimes we wait for the "perfect" moment to get started. However, the time is now. Students are waiting for you to inspire them. Teachers are waiting for you to take them to the next level where they feel empowered to lead students in more intentional ways. More importantly, we live in a nation where social justice continues to be treated as a threat instead of an asset to all of us. The longer we wait, the more students are harmed, and the more teachers and leaders will live in fear of what they can and cannot do, in order to adhere to oppressive educational mandates and policies.

For those of you who are on social media, I encourage you to use the hashtag #SocialJusticeEducation to document how you are teaching, how you are leading, and how students are learning using the framework and activities outlined in this book. I want to bear witness to your teaching/leadership and to continue the conversation beyond the pages of this book. After all, this book was written for you, for me, and for all of us pursuing SJE on a daily basis by any means necessary.

References

Acevedo, N. (2019). Why are migrant children dying in U.S. custody? *NBC News.* https://www.nbcnews.com/news/latino/why-are-migrant-children-dying-u-s-custody-n1010316

ADA.gov. (2020). *Guide to Disability Rights Laws.* https://www.ada.gov/resources/disability-rights-guide/

Alexander, M. (2012). *The new Jim Crow: Mass incarceration in the age of colorblindness.* The New Press.

Alienikoff, T. A. (1991). A case for race-consciousness. *Columbia Law Review,* 91, 1060–1125.

Alvarez, J. (2002). Profile: Julia Alvarez. [Video]. PBS. https://www.pbs.org/video/profile-julia-alvarez/. Accessed on February 2, 2002.

Alvarez, A. (2020). Seeing race in the research on youth trauma and education: A critical review. *Review of Educational Research,* 1–44. https://teachingisintellectual.com/wp-content/uploads/2020/12/Alvarez-2020.pdf

Anderson, R. E., & Stevenson, H. C. (2019). RECASTing racial stress and trauma: Theorizing the healing potential of racial socialization in families. *American Psychologist,* 74, 63–75.

Anti Defamation League. (2021). *Schools are using anti-critical race theory laws to ban children's literature.* https://www.adl.org/resources/blog/schools-are-using-anti-critical-race-theory-laws-ban-childrens-literature?gclid=CjwKCAiAlp2fBhBPEiwA2Q10D44oA9nQI7uLfjUO--LBZe-kiXIzL2Fc--pn1gW0Qnz_SY_HW8HCQxoCQSYQAvD_BwE

Anyon, J. (1980). Social class and the hidden curriculum of work. *Journal of Education,* 67–92. https://www.jstor.org/stable/42741976?seq=1

Armstrong, T. (2017). Neurodiversity: The future of special education? *Association for Supervision and Curriculum Development,* 74, 7. https://www.ascd.org/el/articles/neurodiversity-the-future-of-special-education

Baldwin, J. (1963). A talk to teachers. STS Infrastructures. https://stsinfrastructures.org/content/baldwin-1963-talk-teachers

Banks, J. A. (Ed.). (1996). *Multicultural education, transformative knowledge and action.* Teachers College Press.

Baumer, N., & Freuh, J. (2021). What is neurodiversity? *Harvard Health.* https://www.health.harvard.edu/blog/what-is-neurodiversity-202111232645

Bell, D. (1992). *Faces at the bottom of the well: The permanence of racism.* Basic Books.

Bell, L. A. (2016). *Theoretical foundations for social justice education* (Vol. 3). Routledge.

Belle, C. (2019). What is social justice education anyway? *Education Week.* https://www.edweek.org/teaching-learning/opinion-what-is-social-justice-education-anyway/2019/01

Bennett, C. I. (1995). Preparing teachers for cultural diversity and national standards of academic excellence. *Journal of Teacher Education,* 46(4), 259–265.

Billings, G. L. (2016). Just what is Critical Race Theory and what's it doing in a nice field like education? In Taylor, E., Gillborn, D., & Ladson-Billings, G. (Eds.), *Foundations of Critical Race Theory in education* (pp. 15–30). Routledge.

Brown, A. M. (2017). *Emergent strategy: Shaping change, changing worlds.* AK Press.

Castelli, M. (2023). Introduction to critical race theory and counterstorytelling. *Noise Project.* https://noiseproject.org/introduction-to-critical-race-theory-and-counter-storytelling/

Coates, T. (2015). *Between the world and me.* One World.

Coates, L., & Tresvant, J. (2016). *Special education announcement provides a lesson in social justice.* Office of Special Education and Rehabilitative Services Bog. https://sites.ed.gov/osers/tag/social-justice/

Cochran-Smith, M., & Lytle, S. (1993). *Inside/Outside: Teacher research and knowledge*. Teachers College Press.

Collins, P.H. (2015). Intersectionality's definitional dilemmas. Annual Review of Sociology, 41, 1–20.

Columbia Law School. (2017). Kimberle Crenshaw on intersectionality, more than two decades later. https://www.law.columbia.edu/news/archive/kimberle-crenshaw-intersectionality-more-two-decades-later

Costa, J., & Kalick, B. (1993). Through the lens of a critical friend. *Educational Leadership: Journal of the Department of Supervision and Curriculum Development, N.E.A.* 51(2).

Duvernay, A. (2016). 13th. Netflix. https://www.imdb.com/title/tt5895028/

Enright, J. (2021, August 29). The meaning of neurodiversity: Exploring the significance of the neurodiversity movement. *Medium*. https://medium.com/neurodiversified/what-is-neurodiversity-b0e6e902ef9a

Feldman, J. (2018). *Grading for equity: What it is, why it matters, and how it can transform schools and classrooms*. Corwin.

Fisher, R. M. (2017). Radical love: Is it radical enough? *The International Journal of Critical Pedagogy*, 8(1), 261–281.

Freire, P. (1968). Pedagogy of the Oppressed. Continuum Publishing Company.

Freire, P. (2005). *Teachers as cultural workers: Letters to those who dare to teach* (1st ed.). Westview Press.

Ginwright, S. (2015). *Hope and healing in urban education*. Routledge.

Gogins, K. (2021). Equity leadership model. https://kittygogins.com/home/references/

Gould, S. J. (1981). *The mismeasure of man*. W. W. Norton.

Hammond, Z. (2014). *Culturally responsive teaching and the brain*. Corwin.

Harris, C. I. (2011). Reflections on whiteness as property. *Harvard Law Review*, 133(9), 1710–1791. https://harvardlawreview.org/print/no-volume/whiteness-as-property/

hooks, b. (1994). *Teaching to transgress*. Routledge.

hooks, b. (2000). *All about love*. William Morrow Paperbacks.

Ingraham, C. (2017). The richest 1 percent now owns more of the country's wealth than at any time in the past 50 years. *The Washington Post*. https://www.washingtonpost.com/news/wonk/wp/2017/12/06/the-richest-1-percent-now-owns-more-of-the-countrys-wealth-than-at-any-time-in-the-past-50-years/

Kim, K. H., & Zabellina, D. (2015). Cultural bias in assessment: Can creativity assessment help? *International Journal of Critical Pedagogy*, 129(2).

Knowles, E. D., & Lowery, B. S. (2012). Meritocracy, self-concerns, and whites' denial of racial inequity, self and identity, 11(2), 202–222. https://doi.org/10.1080/15298868.2010.542015

Lareau, A. (2003). *Unequal childhoods*. University of California Press.

Lawrence-Lightfoot, S., & Davis, J. H. (1997). *The art and science of portraiture*. Jossey-Bass.

Leonardo, Z., & Hunter, M. (2007). Imagining the urban: The politics of race, class and schooling. In *The international handbook of urban education* (pp. 779–802). Springer. https://link.springer.com/chapter/10.1007/978-1-4020-5199-9_41

Levin, S. (2023). "It never stops": Killings by US police reach record high in 2022. *The Guardian*. https://www.theguardian.com/us-news/2023/jan/06/us-police-killings-record-number-2022

Lithwick, D. (2020). Unpacking allegations of forced hysterectomies at immigrant detention centers. *Slate*. https://slate.com/news-and-politics/2020/09/hysterectomy-allegation-immigrants-america.html

Lopez, G. (2020). Trump's long history of racism, from the 1970s to 2020. Vox. https://www.vox.com/2016/7/25/12270880/donald-trump-racist-racism-history

Macionis, J. J. (2010). *Sociology* (16th ed.). Pearson.

MacLeod, J. (2008). *Ain't no makin' it*. Westview Press.

Marable, M. (1983). *How capitalism underdeveloped Black America*. South End Press.

McIntosh, K., Moss, E., Nunn, R., & Shambaugh, J. (2020). Examining the black-white wealth gap. *Brookings*. https://www.brookings.edu/blog/upfront/2020/02/27/examining-the-black-white-wealth-gap/

Miller, R., Liu, K., & Ball, A. F. (2020). Critical Counter-Narrative as Transformative Methodology for Educational Equity. *Review of Research in Education, 44*(1), 269–300. https://doi.org/10.3102/0091732X20908501

Mora, R. A. (2014). Key concepts in intercultural dialogue: Counternarratives. https://centerforinterculturaldialogue.files.wordpress.com/2014/10/key-concept-counter-narrative.pdf

Muhammad, G. (2020). *Cultivating genius: An equity framework for culturally and historically responsive literacy.* Scholastic Teaching Resources.

National Center for Education Statistics. (2020). *Source: U.S. Department of Education, Common Core of Data (CCD)—State nonfiscal Survey of public elementary and secondary Education, 2009–10 and 2018–19.* https://nces.ed.gov/ccd/stNfis.asp

National Center for Education Statistics. (2023). *Racial/Ethnic Enrollment in Public Schools. Condition of Education.* U.S. Department of Education, Institute of Education Sciences. https://nces.ed.gov/programs/coe/indicator/cge

National Center for Learning Disabilities. (2020). *Significant disproportionality in Special Education: Current trends and actions for impact.* https://www.ncld.org/wp-content/uploads/2020/10/2020-NCLD-Disproportionality_Trends-and-Actions-for-Impact_FINAL-1.pdf

Neblett, E. W., Sosoo, E. E., Willis, H. A., Bernard, D. L., Bae, J., & Billingsley, J. D. (2016) Racism, racial resilience, and African-American youth development: Person-centered analysis as a tool to promote equity and justice. *Advances in Child Development and Behavior, 51*, 43–79. https://www.sciencedirect.com/science/article/pii/S0065240716300234

Peeples, L. (2020). What the data say about police brutality and racial violence—And which reforms might work. *Nature*. https://www.nature.com/articles/d41586-020-01846-z

Pendakahr, E. (2023). Book bans hit an all time high last year. *Education Week*. https://www.edweek.org/teaching-learning/book-bans-hit-an-all-time-high-last-year/2023/04?s_kwcid=AL!6416!3!602270476281!!!g!!&utm_source=goog&utm_medium=cpc&utm_campaign=ew+dynamic+recent&ccid=dynamic+ads+recent+articles&ccag=recent+articles+dynamic&cckw=&cccv=dynamic+ad&gclid=CjwKCAjwsvujBhAXEiwA_UXnADDpt8lsWo5tjLQFvAo8MM3rRlyoV5dYVOIfBAG5QJa_uZYBvPh28xoCbUoQAvD_BwE

Phoenix, O. (2019). The science of balancing the heart and mind. *The Way of Meditation*. https://www.thewayofmeditation.com.au/the-science-of-balancing-the-heart-and-mind#:~:text=At%20Heart%20Math%20Institution%2C%20recent%20research%20has%20shown,%E2%80%A2%20neurologically%20%28through%20the%20transmission%20of%20nerve%20impulses%29

Pope, D. C. (2003). *Doing school: How we are creating A generation of stressed-out, materialistic, and miseducated students.* Yale University Press.

Safir, S., & Dugan, J. (2021). *Street data: A next generation model for equity, pedagogy and school transformation.* Corwin Press.

Samuel, I., & Wellemeyer, A. (2020). Black students experience racial trauma from racist incidents at school, experts say. *NBC News*. https://www.nbcnews.com/news/nbcblk/black-students-experience-trauma-racist-incidents-school-experts-say-n1232829

Schwartz, S. (2023). Where critical race theory is under attack. *Education Week*. https://www.edweek.org/policy-politics/map-where-critical-race-theory-is-under-attack/2021/06

Semuels, A. (2016). Good school, rich school; Bad school, poor school. *The Atlantic*. https://www.theatlantic.com/business/archive/2016/08/property-taxes-and-unequal-schools/497333/

Sensoy, Ö., & DiAngelo, R. (2017). *Is everyone really equal?: An introduction to key concepts in critical social justice education* (2nd ed.). Teachers College Press.

Shores, K., Kim, H. E., & Still, M. (2019). *Categorical inequality in black and white: Linking disproportionality across multiple educational outcomes.* https://edworkingpapers.com/sites/default/files/ai19-168.pdf

Singleton, G. E. (2021). *Courageous conversations about race: A field guide for achieving equity in schools and beyond.* Corwin Press.

Sleeter, C. E. (1992). Restructuring schools for multicultural education. *Journal of Teacher Education, 43*(2), 141–148.

Stelter, G. (2023). A beginning guide to the 7 chakras and their meanings. *Healthline.* https://www.healthline.com/health/fitness-exercise/7-chakras

Strauss, V. (2015). Big education firms spend millions lobbying for pro-testing policies. *The Washington Post.* https://www.washingtonpost.com/news/answer-sheet/wp/2015/03/30/report-big-education-firms-spend-millions-lobbying-for-pro-testing-policies/

Tiayon, S. B. (2020). How to avoid doing harm when you discuss race at work. https://greatergood.berkeley.edu/article/item/how_to_avoid_doing_harm_when_you_discuss_race_at_work

Trigger tha Gamber. (1996). My crew can't go for that. On The Nutty Professor Soundtrack. Def Jam Recordings.

Tufts University Prison Divestment. (2022). What is the prison industrial complex? https://sites.tufts.edu/prisondivestment/the-pic-and-mass-incarceration/

U.S. Department of Education. (2009, November). *Race to the top program: Executive summary.* https://files.eric.ed.gov/fulltext/ED557422.pdf

Villegas, A. M., & Lucas, T. (2002). Preparing culturally responsive teachers: Rethinking curriculum. *Journal of Teacher Education, 53*(1), 20–32.

White House Archives. (2012). Race to the top. https://obamawhitehouse.archives.gov/issues/education/k-12/race-to-the-top#:~:text=Known%20as%20Race%20to%20the,take%20responsibility%20for%20their%20success

Williams, A. K. (2002). *Being black: Zen and the art of living with fearlessness and grace.* Penguin Books.

Will, M., & Navarro, I. (2022). What is culturally responsive teaching? *Education Week.* https://www.edweek.org/teaching-learning/culturally-responsive-teaching-culturally-responsive-pedagogy/2022/04

Yosso, T. (2005). Whose culture has capital? A critical race theory discussion of community cultural wealth. *Race, Ethnicity and Education, 8*(1), 69–91. https://thrive.arizona.edu/sites/default/files/Whose%20culture%20has%20capital_A%20critical%20race%20theory%20discussion%20of%20community%20cultural%20wealth_1.pdf

Index

social-emotional, 43
Leonardo, Z., 13
Liberation, 39–41
Liberatory pedagogy, 40
Love, 31, 34
   birth and, 6
   chakras, 3, 4 (figure)
   compassion and, 4
   in education, 1
   healing and, 5
   key acts of, 44–45
   parental, 2
   romantic, 1
Luther King, Jr., M., 66

Mainstream students, 90
Marable, M., 49
Maryland State Department of Education (MSDE), 108
McIntosh, K., 69
Medicaid, 69
Meditation, 3
Meritocracy, 59–60
Meritocratic ideology, 79
Morrison, T., 6
Muhammad, Gholdy, 102

Nadia's radical love reflection (RLR), 132–133
Nadia's social justice education testimony, 127–132
National Center for Education Statistics (NCES), 63
National Center for Learning Disabilities, 96
National Council on Disability, 94
National Equity Project, 24
National Urban League, 152
Neblet, Jr., E. W., 65
Neurodiversity terminology, 91 (figure)
New Kid, 67
New York Police Department (NYPD), 114
Nixon, R., 68
No Child Left Behind (NCLB), 88, 92–93

Obama, B., 76, 78
Opportunity, 28, 52, 72, 142, 147
Oppression, 26, 56
   portraiture against, 37–39
   teaching, 17

Parents, 1–2, 44, 49, 65–67, 82, 106, 124, 138–140
Pedagogical reflection, 101–102
Pedagogy, 26, 36, 56
   engaged, 40
   liberatory, 40
   oppressive, 47
Phenomenology, 122
Poetry, 142, 146, 155
Pope, D., 59
Portraiture, 37–39, 42, 50, 119
Post conversation takeaways, 144–148
Power, 7, 19, 21, 34, 39, 126, 133
Predominantly White Institution (PWI), 124
Prison industrial complex (PIC), 96, 97
Prison Policy Institute, 96
Privilege
   imagination and, 12–17
   whiteness, 17
Professional learning communities (PLCs), 105
Public school education policies, 97

Race to the Top (RTT) initiative, 76
Racism, 6, 17, 26, 35, 37, 101, 107
   classism and, 36
   segregation, 64
   socialization, 65
   white supremacy and, 18
Radical love, 1, 3, 5, 15, 25, 34, 86–88
   collective heart, 27–29
   engagement, 39–41
   equity vs. equality barometer, 51–53, 53 (figure)
   gaps vs. inequities, 70–71
   heart chakra histories, 83–84
   key acts of love, 44–45
   tool, for educators, 17–20, 20 (figure)
Radical Love Goal (RLG), 27, 51
"Radical Love: Is It Radical Enough," 18
Radical Love Leadership Community (RLLC), 85
Reflection prompt activity, for teachers, 16
Reflective teaching/learning, 99
Reflexive teaching/learning, 99
Religion, 1, 34
Richard's radical love reflection (RLR), 140
Richard's testimony, 137–139
The RLE Check-In, 39
Romantic love, 1
Ruiz, Y. S., 6